ABOUT THE AUTHOR

Clive George followed a career in industrial management before joining the University of Manchester
to undertake research and consultancy on the use
of impact assessment techniques in international
development. As a Senior Research Fellow in the
University's School of Environment and Development he was principal adviser to the World Bank on
the evaluation and development of impact assessment
systems in the Middle East and North Africa and has
acted as a consultant to the OECD, UNEP and other
international agencies. Through his work for UNEP
and the European Commission he has become one of
the world's leading experts on assessing the interact-
ing economic, social and environmental impacts of
international trade agreements. His books include
Environment and the City (2008) with Peter Roberts
and Joe Ravetz, *Impact Assessment and Sustainable
Development* (2007) with Colin Kirkpatrick and
*Environmental Assessment in Developing and Transitional
Countries* (2000) with Norman Lee. He has published numerous articles on sustainable development,
impact assessment, global governance and international trade.

THE TRUTH ABOUT TRADE

the real impact of liberalization

Clive George

Zed Books

LONDON | NEW YORK

The Truth about Trade: the real impact of liberalization was first published in 2010 by Zed Books Ltd, 7 Cynthia Street, London N1 9JF, UK and Room 400, 175 Fifth Avenue, New York, NY 10010, USA

www.zedbooks.co.uk

Set in Monotype Plantin and Gill Sans Heavy by Ewan Smith, London
Cover designed by David Bradshaw
Printed and bound in Great Britain by the CLE Print Ltd, St Ives, Cambridgeshire

FSC
www.fsc.org
MIX
From responsible sources
FSC® C019549

Distributed in the USA exclusively by Palgrave Macmillan, a division of St Martin's Press, LLC, 175 Fifth Avenue, New York, NY 10010, USA

A catalogue record for this book is available from the British Library
Library of Congress Cataloging in Publication Data available

ISBN 978 1 84813 297 9 hb
ISBN 978 1 84813 298 6 pb
ISBN 978 1 84813 489 8 eb

CONTENTS

BOXES

PREFACE

This book grew out of a ten-year programme of research triggered by mounting opposition to the agenda for the World Trade Organization conference that was to be held in Seattle at the end of 1999. Campaigners for social justice feared that further liberalization of international trade would not end world poverty but increase it. Environmentalists feared that more trade would mean more loss of wildlife, more pollution and more climate change. Trade unionists feared for their members' jobs. Were any of them right to be concerned?

Since the confrontations in Seattle the goal of removing the remaining barriers to international trade has continued to be pursued in the WTO, and increasingly through separate agreements between individual countries or groups of countries. Some progress has been made but less than was hoped. The protesters in Seattle had hoped for the opposite. Neither side can draw much comfort from how the world has changed since then. Poverty has declined in some parts of the world but risen in others. Climate change has accelerated, and the world economy has fallen into its biggest trough since the Second World War. How much of that, if any, might have been due to the trade liberalization measures implemented before Seattle and since? How much might have been avoided if the reforms had proceeded faster? What kind of trade agreements are needed now, if any, to help the world out of crisis?

None of these questions has a simple answer, though many economists believe they do. Many politicians are happy to believe them. They were equally happy to believe that the economic bubble that has just burst was not a bubble. Contemporary economic theory has many uses but many limitations. In seeking answers to the questions the book delves deeper.

Some of the answers come from looking at the numbers. Statistics can tell lies, unmask them, or do no more than indicate whether what they measure is big enough to matter. Much depends on where the numbers come from and how closely we interrogate them. The WTO's own data are as reliable as any.[1] They reveal that few people in the world are now unaffected, for better or worse, by international trade. In 1950 the annual value of world trade was around US$65 billion. By 2007 it was around $14 trillion. While the world economy was growing by a factor of eight, trade grew by a factor of over two hundred. In 1950 total world exports of agricultural and manufactured goods were about 1 per cent of world GDP. By 2007 they were 25 per cent. Trade in services grew even faster, pushing the total up to over 30 per cent. Nearly a third of everything consumed in the world has been imported, while nearly a third of all the goods and services produced are for export.

Further details reveal more. Those numbers are global totals, and hide the fact that some countries are more involved than others. The argument in favour of free trade asserts that developing countries cannot develop unless they remove the barriers that stop them integrating more fully into the global economy. At first sight the numbers seem to support the theory. The most fully integrated country, measured by the combined total of its imports and exports, is Singapore. Like Hong Kong, Singapore imports goods and services with a value more than twice its own GDP. Most of it goes straight back out as exports, which may have something to do with why Singapore has become rich. The country with the least fully integrated economy is Brazil. It imports only about 12 per cent of its GDP and exports only 14 per cent. Brazil is still much poorer than Singapore. So far so good, but then the theory begins to look a little shaky. Fourth from bottom of the list is the European Union, whose imports from the rest of the world are only 15 per cent of its GDP. Its exports are the same as Brazil's at 14 per cent. Third from bottom is Japan. Second from bottom, the least-but-one globally integrated economy in the world, is the USA.

It might seem that America is not the engine of the world economy it is said to be. Other numbers say it is, but only because it is big. Despite being the second most insular of all the world's economies, America is big enough to export more than anyone else and import more than anyone else. In 2007 its imports were valued at $2.4 trillion, followed by Germany with $1.5 trillion, China with $1.3 trillion and Japan with $0.8 trillion. The US economy is nearly as big as the whole of the EU's single market, whose imports from the rest of the world are worth marginally more at $2.5 trillion. Cambodia imports four hundred times less, a mere $6.4 billion. That is not much globally but it is a lot for Cambodia. It is nearly 80 per cent of the country's economy. Its exports are not much less at nearly 70 per cent. Unlike Singapore, Cambodia is not what might be termed a global shopping mall. What it exports is what it produces. Swaziland is similar, with exports worth more than 80 per cent of its economy. Angola's are bigger still, at 87 per cent of its economy. Congo's are even bigger at 93 per cent. Europe's are 14 per cent and America's 11 per cent. Europe and America have achieved their riches without, in their own terms, exporting very much or importing very much. All but a few developing countries export a great deal more, import a great deal more, and remain poor.

Could it possibly be that poor countries are poor not because they trade too little but because they trade too much? Numbers on their own cannot answer that. To get a reasonable understanding of why some countries develop and others do not we have to look wider and deeper, to discover what each of them imports and who consumes it, what it exports and who produces it, what people earn from what they sell, make or grow, and what happens to their prospects of earning more. To get a grasp of whether any of them can develop sustainably we need to look at what the trade does to the natural environment. And then there are the histories of why it is how it is and the politics of how it might change. It is all a bit more complicated than an economic theory.

Most of the book is devoted to the more limited task of assessing the likely impacts of the current trade liberalization agenda on the world's economies, environments and people. In doing so it takes a middle ground between two distinct approaches that are more commonly used. Macro-level econometric studies draw general conclusions about the relationships between trade, growth, incomes and, in some cases, related environmental issues. Empirical studies at the micro-level observe the effects of past trade reforms on households or local environments. Here we combine the two and add a third element, in the political processes through which trade agreements are negotiated. We examine the methods used in econometric studies, identify those aspects which are sufficiently robust to give reliable results, review the empirical research literature to extract general lessons, link the findings within their political context, and draw overall conclusions on the likely economic, social and environmental impacts of each component of the liberalization agenda.

In Part One we see how trade negotiators set about their work, what they negotiate over, and the techniques that have been developed for assessing the consequences. Part Two reports the findings. It examines the impacts of each component of the trade liberalization agenda in turn, covering manufactured goods, agricultural products, all the various types of services, and the rules that prescribe what countries must and must not do in defining their own trade policy. The effects differ considerably between rich countries and poor ones, and have a major influence on the sustainability of development for the world as a whole.

In some respects the impact is positive but in many others it is negative. Some parts of the liberalization agenda reinforce the same economic policies that caused the current global economic crisis. Others inhibit the development of developing countries, accelerate climate change and lead to even faster loss of biological diversity. Part 3 begins by reviewing the minimal extent to which knowledge of the impacts has influenced trade policy. It goes on to develop proposals for more radical changes that would avoid the adverse impacts, maximize the beneficial ones, and help the world climb out of crisis instead of plunging deeper in.

The impacts of international trade can be beneficial or they can be adverse, depending on how it is managed. It can be one of the most effective drivers of human understanding and development, or can be used by the richest and most powerful states for their own gain, with little or no regard for the effects on disadvantaged people in other countries or the integrity of the environment locally and globally. The current world trade agenda offers too little of the first and too much of the second. For the past 300 years it has been driven by Europe and America, initially by one and then by both. That is now changing. The economic power of China, India, Brazil and several other countries is rising rapidly to challenge that of the established players. At the same time the global economy is facing its biggest crisis since the Great Depression and global environmental challenges that have never been faced before. New challenges call for new agendas.

NOTE

1 All the numbers that follow are taken from or derived from WTO, *International Trade Statistics 2008* (www.wto.org/english/res_e/statis_e/ Statis_e.htm) and the World Bank's *World Development Report 2009*. WTO statistics website accessed 30 May 2009.

ACKNOWLEDGEMENTS

Of the many people without whom this book would not have been possible, Colin Kirkpatrick stands out, first for giving me the opportunity to join him in working on the trade impact studies and then for all the encouragement, support, ideas and friendship that followed. Colin combines a deep understanding of development economics with an inquisitive mind and a human warmth that I have valued immensely. Both of us owe a debt of gratitude to Norman Lee, which in my case extends equally to Christopher Wood. Norman and Chris were among the pioneers of environmental impact assessment in Europe and globally, and it was a great privilege to work with them both. Norman's subsequent work with Colin on integrated economic, social and environmental assessment laid the foundations for the research programme on which the book is based.

The book draws on the work of many other colleagues in Manchester University and its partner institutions, all of whose contributions are gratefully acknowledged. They include Balsam Ahmad, Sergio Alessandrini, Carlo Altomonte, Julian Arkell, Ron Bisset, Michel Bouchard, Carol Chouchani Cherfane, Julian Clarke, Raymond Colley, Lyn Currie, Mauricio López Dardaine, Maximiliano López Dardaine, Mahrukh Doctor, Annie Dufey, Simon Evenett, Guillermo Flichman, Doug Flint, Jennifer Franz, Ian Gillson, Andrew Grainger, Kevin Gray, Peter Greenhalgh, Maryanne Grieg-Gran, Bénédicte Hermelin, Leonith Hinojosa, Tomasz Iwanow, Larbi Jaidi, Michael Johnson, Carys Jones, Marko Katila, Ulrich Kleih, Géraldine Kutas, Jacob Lind Ramskov, Alan Marter, Fernando Masi, Diana Mitlin, Oliver Morrissey, Victor Murinde, Rachid Nafti, Peter Nelson, Hanna Norberg, Joe Ravetz, Pedro Regina, Lydia Richardson, Matt Ryder, Serban Scrieciu, Maria Belen Servín, Markku Simula, Dirk Willem te Velde, Martin Hvidt Thelle, Kenneth Westlake and Steve Wiggins.

Among these I would particularly like to thank Oliver Morrissey and Dirk Willem te Velde for many stimulating debates, as well as their specialist inputs on key topics. Others to whom I owe special thanks are Carol Chouchani Cherfane, whose untiring enthusiasm and intimate knowledge of the region played a vital role in the studies for the Mediterranean countries, and Lyn Currie, who coordinated the whole programme with such skill and good cheer. Among the people in other organizations that have undertaken trade impact studies for the European Commission, I would like to thank in particular Jochen Krimphoff, Sarah Richardson and Nicolas Boudeville of the team at PricewaterhouseCoopers, for the spirit with which they shared ideas as well as for the studies on which the book has drawn.

Of the many people in the European Commission to whom I owe a debt of gratitude I would like to thank in particular Robert Madelin, who turned an imaginative idea into a reality, Rupert Schlegelmilch, who built on that foundation, and Eric Peters and Nadia de Brito Pires, whose untiring efforts kept the whole programme going. Their skill and good humour made even the most challenging debates a pleasure to take part in. Despite our many disagreements, having the opportunity to subject the Commission's policies to independent public scrutiny was a great privilege. The views expressed here are those of the author alone, and do not in any way represent those of the Commission or any of its staff. I express my appreciation also to the many people in non-governmental organizations who made vital contributions to the programme, with particular thanks to Gidon Bromberg, Eugene Clancy, Nishant Pandey, Charly Poppe, Keith Tyrell and Vanya Walker-Leigh for their constructive criticisms and support.

Of the many other people with whom I have had the opportunity to exchange ideas on trade issues I have been particularly influenced by the insights of Frank Ackerman, Richard Auty, Paul Ekins, Konrad von Moltke, Sheila Page, Sandra Polaski, Ron Steenblik and Mark Weisbrot. Each has made key contributions to understanding the links between the economic, social and environmental effects of international trade and the rules that govern it. Among my colleagues in the International Association for Impact Assessment I am especially grateful to Hussein Abaza, Michel Bouchard, Bernice Goldsmith, Jan Joost Kessler, Rachel McCormick, Jo Treweek and Orlando Venn, all of whose ideas and support have been very much appreciated.

In drawing it all together in the book I give special thanks to Ellen Hallsworth, whose enthusiasm from the start gave me great cheer, to Ken Barlow for his much welcomed editorial guidance and suggestions, and to Ruvani de Silva and the other members of the production and marketing team at Zed Books for their highly professional work in bringing it to fruition. For helping to turn my impenetrable prose into something more readable I am indebted to our daughter Clare, a far more accomplished author than I will ever be. My biggest thank-you of all is to Kay, my wife and very special friend, for far more than putting up with my long hours of typing, retyping and then starting again. Without her encouragement and support there would be no book.

ABBREVIATIONS

ACP	Africa, Caribbean and Pacific
CBD	Convention on Biological Diversity
DSM	Dispute Settlement Mechanism
DSU	Dispute Settlement Understanding
EC	European Commission
EIA	environmental impact assessment
EU	European Union
FDI	foreign direct investment
FTA	free trade area
GATS	General Agreement on Trade in Services
GATT	General Agreement on Tariffs and Trade
GDP	gross domestic product
GPA	Government Procurement Agreement
IA	impact assessment
IMF	International Monetary Fund
IPCC	Intergovernmental Panel on Climate Change
IPR	intellectual property rights
ITC	International Trade Centre
LDC	least developed country
MEA	multilateral environmental agreement
MFN	most favoured nation
NAFTA	North American Free Trade Agreement
NEPA	National Environmental Policy Act
NGO	non-governmental organization
OECD	Organisation for Economic Co-operation and Development
RIA	regulatory impact assessment
RTA	regional trade agreement
SDT	special and differential treatment
SIA	sustainability impact assessment
SME	small/medium-sized enterprise
SPS	Sanitary and Phytosanitary Measures
TBT	Technical Barriers to Trade

TRIMs	Trade-Related Investment Measures
TRIPs	Trade-Related aspects of Intellectual Property Rights
UN	United Nations
UNCTAD	United Nations Conference on Trade and Development
UNDP	United Nations Development Programme
UNEP	United Nations Environment Programme
UPOV	Union for the Protection of New Varieties of Plants
WCO	World Customs Organization
WIPO	World Intellectual Property Organization
WTO	World Trade Organization

ONE | **AGENDAS**

INTRODUCTION

Since the late eighteenth and early nineteenth centuries the arguments for and against free trade have tended to be aligned with the strategic goals of particular countries or the more immediate interests of influential groups within them. When Britain was the dominant industrial power it stood to gain from allowing unrestricted imports of raw materials and commodities, while persuading other countries to remove all their barriers to its manufactured exports. Other countries' efforts to catch up were better served by policies that were more selective in what they chose to import from their number-one competitor. Even in Britain opinion was divided. The new industrial elite stood to gain, both from higher exports of its products and from the lower cost of feeding its workforce with cheap imported food. The country's landowning gentry stood to lose. Similar factors still apply. While economists continue to debate the theoretical benefits of free trade, and civil society groups express their concerns for the social and environmental consequences, the actual process of negotiating trade agreements revolves around the short- or long-term interests of individual countries and of influential factions within each.

Chapter 1 begins by exploring the background to the trade impact assessment studies on which this book is based, and goes on to review the historical debates over the relationships between trade liberalization, economic growth, poverty, environmental degradation and sustainable development. In Chapter 2 we examine the process through which trade agreements are negotiated, both in the WTO and in regional and bilateral agreements. Chapter 3 describes the impact assessment techniques that have been used to evaluate the impacts, as originally introduced in America and subsequently adopted in environmental legislation throughout the world, and how they have been adapted and extended to evaluate the economic, social and environmental impacts of trade liberalization.

1 | FROM THE CORN LAWS TO SEATTLE

The proposal of any new law or regulation of commerce which comes from this order [those who live by profit] ought always to be listened to with great precaution, and ought never to be adopted till after having been long and carefully examined, not only with the most scrupulous, but with the most suspicious attention. It comes from an order of men whose interest is never exactly the same with that of the public, who have generally an interest to deceive and even to oppress the public, and who accordingly have, upon many occasions, both deceived and oppressed it. (Smith 1904 [1776]: 222)

The term trade liberalization describes the process through which countries negotiate and agree to ever tighter and more extensive rules of international trade. Adam Smith would not have approved. As an advocate of free trade he was deeply suspicious of any law or regulation introduced to govern it. In Smith's view any trade rules proposed by commercial organizations warranted particular scrutiny, for what were liable to be deceitful attempts to increase their own profits at the expense of the general public.

Proponents of the current trade liberalization agenda claim that it is essential for globally sustainable development. This chapter begins with a review of the background to the research programme through which that claim has been evaluated. It goes on to examine the history of the sustainable development idea, and the even longer history of arguments for and against free trade. The classical economists of the eighteenth and nineteenth centuries were sharply divided in their views on the economic effects, with varying attitudes to the social and environmental ones. Their neoclassical successors have avoided the problems by taking a different approach. After reviewing the arguments the chapter concludes with a brief summary of the approach taken in the rest of the book.

THE BATTLE IN SEATTLE

In December 1999, the last month of the last year of the last century of the last millennium, the drive for what is called free trade was brought to a halt in a blaze of publicity. At the end of the previous month ministers and senior government officials from all around the world had met in Seattle to launch a new round of negotiations in the World Trade Organization, to be known as the Millennium Round. It never took place. The conference ended in chaos, with protesters blocking the streets and delegates from poor countries rejecting the proposals presented by rich ones.

Since the 'battle in Seattle' opinion has been divided on whether free trade is fair trade, and whether it helps or hinders efforts to reduce world poverty and halt unsustainable exploitation of the natural environment. One side of this debate takes the view that trade liberalization is essential for sustained growth of the global economy, that this growth drives the development of developing countries, and that it increases the resources available for protecting the environment. The other side argues that the growth due to trade has been unevenly spread between countries, that it has been associated with widening income gaps in both poor countries and rich ones, and that it has had damaging effects on the natural environment both locally and globally. The liberalization of world trade is seen on the one hand as being an essential component of sustainable development, and on the other as being detrimental to it. Intermediate positions argue that international trade can make a positive contribution to sustainable development, but that the opposite can occur if the rules by which trade is governed are inappropriate.

During the preparations for the Seattle conference the European Commission embarked on an ambitious attempt to clarify the issues. On the initiative of Trade Commissioner Pascal Lamy (later to become Director General of the WTO), an independent study was commissioned to assess the effects of the Seattle proposals on sustainable development. The study, known as a sustainability impact assessment (SIA), would show how big the benefits were and whether the public concerns were justified. Through a combination of consultative processes and technical analysis it aimed to contribute to a public dialogue that would, if possible, defuse the arguments. That first attempt achieved little. In terms of heading off the Seattle confrontation it achieved nothing. The study was of necessity highly superficial, having been rushed through in the few months leading up to the conference. It did no more than confirm that the potential benefits were genuine and that many of the opposing concerns were equally genuine (Kirkpatrick et al. 1999). Anything more useful would need a fuller examination.

After the failure of the Seattle conference the idea of evaluating the complex impacts of trade agreements before they are agreed was put on ice, until the WTO regrouped to revive the negotiations at the 2001 Ministerial Conference in Doha. Unlike Seattle in the USA, Doha, in the Gulf state of Qatar, is not an easy place to get into for banner-waving protesters. In parallel with the choice of location, European and American trade officials had taken note of the objections to the Seattle proposals and had amended them accordingly. The Doha agenda would be a development agenda, with the needs of low-income countries to the fore, along with the need for development to be environmentally sustainable. The conference proceeded smoothly, agreement was reached, and the Doha Round of negotiations began. Commissioner Lamy's idea of undertaking sustainability impact assessments of the likely consequences was revived as well, now with sufficient time and resources to examine the issues in more depth.

The cost of the Seattle study, including the amount spent on background research and developing the methodology, was about a hundred thousand euros. Since then the EC has spent around ten million euros on trade SIAs, accounting for about 10 per cent of the annual budget of its Directorate General for Trade (European Commission 2003a). Nearly one and a half million euros have been devoted to assessing the impacts of the WTO Doha agenda, with the rest spent on similar studies of Europe's bilateral and regional trade agreements with individual countries or groups of countries. The level of expenditure reflects a decision of the European Council at its 2001 meeting in Göteborg, which committed the European Commission to assessing the impacts of all major policy proposals on globally sustainable development (European Commission 2001a), with particular emphasis on trade agreements (European Commission 2003b).

The impacts identified by these studies are many and complex. Some are good for some people but bad for others. Other impacts have the opposite effect. Some are good for some aspects of the natural environment while others are bad for other aspects. Most of the effects vary according to what policies governments choose to adopt in parallel. Throughout the SIA programme civil society organizations have kept on asking for an overall result. They want as much detail as they can get, but what is the bottom line? Are the proposals good or bad? Do the negotiated trade agreements make a positive contribution to sustainable development or a negative one? None of the studies has attempted to answer that question. We shall do here. We make use of the findings in such a way as to fill the gap.

SUSTAINABLE DEVELOPMENT

The idea of sustainable development emerged in the 1970s from a growing fear that the established pattern of development was approaching limits that would force it to a halt through major damage to local and global environments. Many scientists feared that the greenhouse gases produced from burning fossil fuels and other anthropogenic sources might cause catastrophic climate change, and were warning of similar effects from continuing loss of biological diversity. By 1972 these and other concerns had grown sufficiently serious for governments to meet in Stockholm at the United Nations Conference on the Human Environment. The background report for the conference argued that 'technological man' was 'on a course which could alter dangerously, and perhaps irreversibly, the natural systems of his planet upon which his biological survival depends', while most of the world's population had still 'hardly raised their claims on the planet above those of neolithic man' (Ward and Dubos 1972: 46–7). During the conference India's prime minister Indira Gandhi reminded delegates that the claims of the world's poor should not be overridden by the environmental concerns of the rich. 'Of all the pollutants we face,' she argued, 'the worst is poverty – we want more development' (Sandbrook 1992: 16).

The subsequent quest for a new form of development that would be environmentally sustainable led to the World Conservation Strategy of 1980 and the 1987 report of the World Commission on Environment and Development, chaired by Norway's premier Gro Harlem Brundtland. The Brundtland report, *Our Common Future*, had a dramatic effect in raising public awareness of the need for sustainable development (World Commission on Environment and Development 1987). The ideas that it expressed were subsequently elevated to the level of international agreements at the Rio Earth Summit of 1992 (the UN Conference on Environment and Development). This went a long way towards defining how sustainable development might become a practical reality, through its overarching Rio Declaration and the detailed proposals of Agenda 21, the Convention on Biological Diversity and the Framework Convention on Climate Change.

The follow-up conference held in Johannesburg in 2002 (the UN Conference on Sustainable Development) reported the same concerns as had been expressed three decades earlier at Stockholm in 1972 and then again at Rio de Janeiro in 1992. Little has changed since. Biological diversity is still declining, climate change has progressed from a concern to a reality, and the needs of the world's poor have still not been met. Sustainable development is proving to be an elusive goal. Meanwhile, opinion remains divided on whether international trade agreements are part of the solution or part of the problem.

TRADE LIBERALIZATION

The trade agreements that are forged in the WTO or through regional and bilateral negotiations are among the main drivers of economic globalization, through which the world economy has become increasingly integrated. The food that we eat, the clothes that we wear and the cars that we drive now come from anywhere in the world. The income from our savings and pension funds can come from anywhere too. Goods and capital both move around the world with little restraint, though still not as freely as they might. Trade agreements aim to reduce the remaining barriers and ultimately eliminate them, to extend international trade even further.

The economic case for free trade rests mainly on the economic theory that any interference with the free market economy reduces its efficiency and stops it achieving what would otherwise be an optimal distribution of scarce resources. Trade economists refer to any impediment to free trade as a trade distortion, which has to be removed if the perfect outcomes of a perfect market are to be achieved. Trade liberalization also has other theoretical benefits. The removal of a trade barrier results in an increase in trade, so that continually reducing the barriers produces continually increasing trade. This contributes to global economic growth, for as long as it takes for all the barriers to be removed. Once the barriers have all gone there can be no further gains, but until that point is reached everyone should, in theory, benefit. If every country's trade grows in the same proportion as global trade, its economy will grow in the same proportion as the global economy. One of the many tasks of sustainability impact assessment is to assess the extent to which these theories apply in practice.

Trade negotiations aim to reduce or eliminate import taxes, export taxes, legal and administrative restrictions on either imports or exports, and any kind of subsidy for products or services that can be traded internationally. All of these impediments to perfectly free trade hamper other countries' economic ambitions and impose some form of economic cost on the country that applies them. This is the price of obtaining whatever benefits they confer. Trade barriers are introduced for a wide variety of economic, social or environmental reasons. Social and environmental reasons include preserving the character of rural areas, ensuring the security of food supplies, promoting equitable income distribution, generating government revenues for social, environmental or other expenditure, or, just as commonly, responding to the demands of powerful interest groups. Economic reasons generally relate to a country's long-term goals for its economic development, which may outweigh the shorter-term costs of forgoing cheap imports or subsidizing domestic production.

The costs and benefits of barriers to free trade have been a hot topic ever since the arguments for and against repeal of the British Corn Laws in the late eighteenth and early nineteenth centuries. Adam Smith played an important role in the debate. As can be seen from the quotation at the beginning of this chapter, Smith was less of an enthusiast for the workings of the free market than is widely assumed. Nevertheless, despite his distrust of the profit-seeking motives of international traders, he decided that in this case they were right. Smith joined the debate on the side of repeal, followed by the second of the great classical economists, David Ricardo. Thanks in part to their advocacy, the protectionist laws governing Britain's agricultural trade were eventually abolished in 1846. The reforms occurred in parallel with the Industrial Revolution, reflecting a progressive transfer of influence from the country's landowning gentry to its newly emerging business elite. They made an important contribution to Britain's transformation from a largely agricultural economy into the world's dominant industrial and commercial trading power.

As well as supporting the abolition of British agricultural protectionism, Ricardo promoted the argument that other countries would benefit from removing their barriers to Britain's industrial exports. He showed how, as well as consumers benefiting from cheap imports, entrepreneurs in all countries would obtain higher profits if the market were allowed to steer investment towards their most competitive industries. It was this principle of comparative advantage, he argued, 'which determines that wine shall be made in France and Portugal, that corn shall be grown in America and Poland, and that hardware and other goods shall be manufactured in England' (Ricardo 2001 [1821]: 90). The German economist Friedrich List was unconvinced. He accepted that this would be a consequence of free trade, but not that it would benefit any country but England. He countered Ricardo's advocacy with the observation that

> any nation which by means of protective duties and restrictions on navigation has raised her manufacturing power and her navigation to such a degree of development that no other nation can sustain free competition with her, can do nothing wiser than to throw away these ladders of her greatness, to preach to other nations the benefits of free trade. (List 1885 [1841]: 252)

List's own preaching was no more altruistic than Ricardo's. He was an even stronger advocate of German imperialism than Ricardo was of the

English version. Similar economic arguments to theirs, for the removal of trade barriers by other countries and against accepting the advice, continue to this day.

TRADE, ENVIRONMENT AND POVERTY

Neither David Ricardo nor Friedrich List was unduly concerned about the social and environmental effects of expanding world trade and global economic growth. Both sided with Karl Marx in condemning the gloomier analysis of Thomas Malthus. This suggested that the combination of population growth and environmental constraints would make it impossible for economic growth ever to eliminate world poverty. John Stuart Mill sided with Malthus. He proposed alternative principles of political economy which, he believed, would allow perpetual improvement in the quality of human life while conserving the natural environment.

As the strongest advocate of individual liberties among the classical economists, Mill was also a strident environmental conservationist. He drew little satisfaction from

> contemplating the world with nothing left to the spontaneous activity of nature; with every rood of land brought into cultivation, which is capable of growing food for human beings; every flowery waste or natural pasture ploughed up, all quadrupeds or birds which are not domesticated for man's use exterminated as his rivals for food, every hedgerow or superfluous tree rooted out, and scarcely a place left where a wild shrub or flower could grow without being eradicated as a weed in the name of improved agriculture. (Mill 1909 [1848]: bk 4, ch. 6)

In a foretaste of the arguments that would arise 150 years later, Mill suggested that 'it must always have been seen, more or less distinctly, by political economists, that the increase of wealth is not boundless: that at the end of what they term the progressive state lies the stationary state'. He traced the roots of Malthusian pessimism to the arguments of Adam Smith, and expressed the hope that his successors would 'be content to be stationary long before necessity compels them to it'.

Neoclassical economic theory escapes the problems foreseen by the classical theories of Smith, Ricardo, List, Malthus, Marx and Mill by shifting the emphasis from the production of goods and services to the behaviour of consumer demand. If demand outstrips supply prices rise, reducing demand for resources as they become scarce and stimulating growth in other economic sectors that are less constrained. Perpetual economic growth then becomes possible, with the structure of the economy changing in response to environmental change. When oil has been consumed to the extent that it is no longer extractable at an affordable price, growing demand for it is replaced by growing demand for something else. This something else might not yet exist, but would emerge automatically in response to the price signals. There may be considerable time lags between an environmental effect, a price signal and a market response to it. This may result in significant overshoot before the neoclassical theory can take effect.

Classical, neoclassical and other economic theories play an important role in assessing the likely impacts of a trade agreement. Each has its own uses, alongside many other sources of understanding of how people, economies and environments interact with each other. Sustainability impact assessment is a highly multidisciplinary task. Drawing it all together is a jack-of-all-trades task. We will not be delving into any of it in any great depth here. Rather, the aim is to share the insights that have emerged from the assessments, present and interpret their main findings, and consider the implications for future policies.

2 | A MATTER FOR NEGOTIATION

The most extensive public benevolence which can commonly be exerted with any considerable effect is that of the statesmen, who project and form alliances among neighbouring or not very distant nations, for the preservation either of what is called the balance of power, or of the general peace and tranquillity of the states within the circle of their negotiations. The statesmen, however, who plan and execute such treaties, have seldom anything in view but the interest of their respective countries. (Smith 1982 [1759]: 241)

Some of the sharpest lessons of the trade impact assessment studies have come not from examining the impacts of trade agreements but from talking to Europe's negotiators and their counterparts in other countries, observing some of their debates, and taking part in their dialogue with other government officials and civil society representatives.

In this chapter we begin by examining the objectives of the European Commission in launching its sustainability impact assessment programme. We then look at the process through which trade agreements are negotiated, both in the World Trade Organization and in preferential agreements between individual countries or regional groups. We conclude with a discussion of the role the impact assessment studies have played in this process, and the extent to which they have been able to take an independent stance.

A QUESTION FOR THE TRADE COMMISSIONER

The WTO negotiations that were launched at the Doha conference proceeded in fits and starts. At the next inter-ministerial meeting at Cancún in Mexico they collapsed, before stuttering back to life to reach another impasse in Hong Kong at the end of 2005. By then Peter Mandelson (now Lord Mandelson) had replaced Pascal Lamy as Europe's Commissioner for Trade. In the following March he expressed his own concerns about free trade to an international conference to review the SIA programme, for both the stalled WTO negotiations and Europe's regional and bilateral agreements. To a somewhat surprised audience the Commissioner observed that there is no automatic rule that trade liberalization will lead to greater economic growth, never mind long term sustainability. It can certainly lead to acute short term adjustment costs, as I've seen in my mandate among textile producers and leather shoe manufacturers, not to mention Mauritian sugar growers and Caribbean banana producers. Whether the short term pain is balanced by a long term gain depends on many different factors. (European Commission 2006a: 1)

After describing how the impact assessment studies aimed to identify those factors and the actions that would be needed to ensure beneficial outcomes, the Commissioner sat down to enthusiastic applause.

When the other keynote speeches had been delivered an arm clad in vivid fuchsia shot up in the air at the best strategic location in the auditorium, in the middle of the third or fourth row of packed seats. It belonged to a journalist of some considerable experience whose tactics won the chair's eye and the first question. After complimenting Mr Mandelson on his speech she asked whether he would be saying the same thing in Marrakesh the following week in the negotiations on the Euro-Mediterranean Free Trade Area. In particular, would he be warning the other delegates of the potentially adverse impacts in their countries which had been identified in the impact assessment report? The answer, barely disguised in politician-speak, was a simple no. The Commissioner explained why. He would not be going to Marrakesh to negotiate on behalf of Morocco, nor the other countries on the southern and eastern shores of the Mediterranean. The report would be available to his counterparts on the other side of the table, but only they could decide what negotiating positions to adopt in the interests of their own countries. Europe's Trade Commissioner would be negotiating for Europe.

Pascal Lamy had said much the same when promoting the SIA programme three years before. In response to criticism that the assessment of impacts in other countries might be regarded by the governments of those countries as an intrusion, he explained that the European Commission was simply trying to ensure that Europe's negotiators were sufficiently well informed to take account of the collective preferences of European citizens (European Commission 2003a). Some of those citizens would prefer European policy to have no adverse impacts on people and environments elsewhere in the world, while others would prefer an extra euro in the pocket. Like Peter Mandelson, Commissioner Lamy would take the SIA findings into account as he saw fit, in the process of negotiating for Europe.

Few if any European citizens get very agitated about the impact of EU trade policy on the USA. Their concerns are for the impacts of European policy on countries that are less well equipped to promote their own economic interests, protect the poorer sections of their societies or manage their natural environment effectively. They fear that these countries' economies may be harmed more than helped, poverty made higher instead of lower, and development even less environmentally sustainable. Further concerns arise when common global or regional interests go unrecognized within the economic bargaining processes of trade negotiations. Climate change and loss of biodiversity may be accelerated instead of slowed and stopped.

Pascal Lamy was well aware of these issues when he initiated the SIA programme, as were most of his negotiators. Not all took them very seriously. Most of the negotiators that those of us involved in the SIA programme met in the early days were downright antagonistic, seeing the whole programme as an exceedingly irksome public relations exercise. It took us, as a group of academics with a background in impact assessment and sustainable development, quite a while to learn about the niceties of trade negotiations. We would never have survived the first six months had it not been for the sublime skills of Robert Madelin, a former chief negotiator himself, who had been asked by Lamy to take charge of the SIA programme, or, possibly, had originated the idea and sowed it in his Commissioner's mind. Madelin was far too adroit ever to reveal his true motives for anything, but my best guess is that his concerns for sustainable development were totally genuine. This was certainly the case for one member of Europe's negotiating team. At our first meeting, in private, she expressed the hope that the SIA studies would prove sufficiently conclusive to hold her back from doing what she was paid to do.

THE NEGOTIATION PROCESS

Trade negotiations are precisely that, negotiations. They would not take anything like as long as they do if the world were as simple as the mathematical equations used by trade economists. Every gain that each country hopes to make would be given a dollar value, as would every loss it wishes to avoid. The mathematical analysis would yield an optimal solution in which no country experiences a net loss and all maximize their net gains. The solution is remarkably simple. No matter what tolerably credible numbers are put into the equations, the optimum occurs when every country removes all its barriers to free trade. Having recognized that simple truth the negotiators would all go home, redundant. If any country chose not join in it would not deter the rest. The biggest gains to each country come from unilateral removal of its own trade barriers, no matter what the others do. As Nobel Prize-winning economist Paul Krugman has pointed out, if the conventional economic argument in favour of free trade were the only consideration there would be no WTO and no trade negotiations (Krugman 1997).

In reality these economic calculations play only a minor role in the development of a country's negotiating position. They clearly show that America and Europe would benefit from removing all their agricultural subsidies and import barriers, irrespective of other countries' actions. Yet they will not do it, other than as a minor concession here or there in return for other countries responding to their requests. The same calculations show that those countries would benefit just as much from doing what they are asked, even without the concessions. They too will not do it, unless they can get something in return. Each party uses the calculations of net economic benefit liberally in its efforts to influence the policies of other parties, and hardly at all in developing its own. Other factors are far more important.

If policy-makers do their job thoroughly they pay special attention to identifying which industries, new or old, will be crucial for the country's future development and which can be allowed to decline and die. The task is never easy. One of the reasons that Europe and America refuse to let their agriculture go into decline is that large landowners tend to be highly influential people, alongside the problems caused by small ones when they block the roads with tractors. But that is not the only reason. There are a host of other equally strong motives for maintaining trade barriers or removing them, promoted by many other equally influential people with equally powerful interests.

Roughly half the key economic actors in each country call for greater access to other countries' markets, for the sake of the extra jobs. The extra profits would not go amiss either. The other half demand protection of their own markets, and forecast dire consequences if they lose it. In developing a negotiating position policy-makers take all the competing interests into account, talking directly to the people with the greatest power and considering the views of any others who might influence the result of the next election. In countries with highly developed democratic institutions no section of the public can be ignored. Elsewhere the main influence on negotiating positions, and often the only influence, comes from the major commercial players. Their interests may be aligned with those of their workforces and the rest of the population, or may not. Once all the relevant interests have been consulted and an adequate level of consensus has been achieved, a negotiating mandate is prepared that tells negotiators what to ask for and what they can offer in return. Then the manoeuvring begins.

Even bilateral negotiations between just two countries can get quite complex. More often than not one party or the other, or both, is similarly engaged in parallel negotiations with other trading partners over granting each other similarly favourable status, all of which interacts with what might be agreed with someone else. At the same time the same countries are negotiating over the same issues in the multilateral framework of the WTO. Here there are over 150 countries to deal with, each with its own markets to be tapped, each with its own industries to be defended, each of which has to accept every detail of all the multifaceted aspects of a proposed agreement before it can be signed. Every country's efforts to advance its own commercial interests have to contend with those of every other. Coalitions are formed, efforts to break them are made, agendas are changed and negotiating positions are revised, sometimes without opposing groups even noticing (Odell 2006). International NGOs make their presence felt as much as the organizational arrangements allow, stirring up media stories, exposing the worst of the stupidities and, occasionally, embarrassing negotiators into withdrawing their claims.

In working towards some kind of conclusion each country has its own view of what development means and what sustainable development means. What it achieves is what it succeeds in negotiating.

THE ROLE OF SUSTAINABILITY IMPACT ASSESSMENT

When Pascal Lamy introduced the SIA programme it was not with the aim of helping Europe develop its negotiating positions. If all the various analyses that are used to develop a negotiating position were made public, and therefore accessible to other countries' negotiators, the EC would put itself at a considerable disadvantage in the negotiations. The same applies to the USA and every other country. None is foolish enough to reveal its hand to the people it is negotiating with. The SIA studies are not intended to influence the negotiations directly through the negotiating mandate, but indirectly through the public dialogue on implementing that mandate. No one but policy-makers and negotiators knows what the mandate is, other than through what is revealed as the negotiations proceed. The views of interested parties are taken into account when the mandate is prepared, and then again as each country's requests, counter-requests and responses emerge. The SIA studies aim to provide objective and reasonably factual information for the subsequent debate between policy-makers and civil society as they work towards an eventual agreement.

When the EC initiated the SIA studies in 1999 it was part of its effort to counter mounting opposition to the Seattle proposals from a wide range of civil society groups. It was expected that an independent, objective analysis would demonstrate that many of the concerns were unfounded, while highlighting any others for which a response might be needed. This could be through a change to the proposed trade agreement or through the adoption or amendment of appropriate parallel measures. The overall aim was to allay the worst of the fears and strengthen public support for Europe's trade policy.

There is more to European, American and other countries' trade policies than haggling over their competing commercial interests. There would be no haggling at all if it were possible to go directly to the idealized goal of totally free trade. In that ideal the WTO's rules would be much the same as those of the European Union's single market, such that countries would have only one simple decision to make. To join or not to join. For trade between any WTO member and every other there would be no tariffs, no barriers behind the borders, and no borders. Goods, services and capital would all move freely, and so would people. The last are by far the most problematic. Without free movement of the biggest and most important factor of production, labour, so-called free trade is inevitably reduced to haggling over how far each country is prepared to go with all the rest. There are good reasons for going quite a long way, irrespective of any commercial advantage that might be won through the process of give and take.

One reason, real or claimed, is economic efficiency. Another is the stability of the whole world trading system. Whatever other role the WTO might be given or might assume, its most important task is to stop trade wars. The lower the tariff levels that are bound by an agreement, the less scope countries have to inflict damage on each other's export industries by suddenly raising them. Other WTO rules play a similar role, but can be highly asymmetrical in their different effects on different countries. Other asymmetries are inherent in the different types of goods and services that different countries import and export. All these asymmetrical effects can be alleviated or locked in place according to the details of the rules that are agreed. Any attempt to change the rules typically leads to yet more haggling.

In such circumstances the civil society organizations that took to the streets in Seattle would have had no faith whatsoever in the SIA studies if they had been carried out by the European Commission itself, as one of the major interested parties in the negotiations. Even when undertaken by supposedly independent organizations, the fact that they were paid for by the EC would leave their credibility suspect. This was a big issue when we were deciding whether or not to get involved beyond the initial stage of developing the methodology (see Chapter 3). To a large extent it was the EC's acceptance of that methodology which tipped the balance. The proposed approach was the brainchild of Manchester economist Norman Lee, who had played a key role in developing the EU directive through which impact assessment techniques had been introduced into every member state's environmental legislation some years before. Its cornerstone was transparency and public accountability. Some or all of the SIA reports might still be biased in favour of the EC, but if they were, every aspect of their analysis would be wide open to public criticism.

We have had plenty of that.[1] We have had plenty from the European Commission too.[2] On balance we can claim to have stood in the middle of the road for several years without ever quite getting run down.

3 | CLAIMS AND COUNTER-CLAIMS

The man scarce lives who is not more credulous than he ought to be, and who does not, upon many occasions, give credit to tales which not only turn out to be perfectly false, but which a very moderate degree of reflection and attention might have taught him could not well be true. (Smith 1982 [1759]: 325)

Trade policy-makers are not unique in overstating the benefits of their proposals while understating or completely ignoring any adverse effects. Advocates of any development proposal may do the same, particularly for impacts on the natural environment. Growing awareness of the need for sustainable development led to the introduction of techniques for assessing the impacts of such proposals before they are approved, initially in the USA and subsequently in most of the rest of the world. The trade impact assessment studies made use of these techniques, extended to cover social and economic impacts as well as environmental ones, in all the countries affected.

In this chapter we begin by summarizing the history of impact assessment and its applications. We then examine the extent to which the approach can be misused, not to provide evidence on which to base decisions, but to create a veneer of evidence in support of decisions that have already been made. After looking at ways in which this can be avoided we examine the methodology developed for the European Commission's sustainability impact assessments of trade policy, and the particular techniques employed. The chapter concludes with a brief discussion of how the evidence on the impacts of trade liberalization is explored in the rest of the book.

IMPACT ASSESSMENT

At the beginning of the brightly optimistic 1960s Rachel Carson's book *Silent Spring* warned that all was not as bright as it seemed. Defenders of business as usual like to point out that despite her concerns the cheerily singing American robin did not become extinct. Environmentalists reply that Carson's book was one of the reasons why it didn't. By the end of the decade America had put a man on the moon and passed the National Environmental Policy Act of 1969, described as 'the most far reaching environmental and conservation measure ever enacted by the Congress' (Wood 2003: 18).

The influence of NEPA reached far beyond the United States. The requirement to assess the environmental impacts of development proposals before they are approved spread rapidly across the world, along with appropriate processes and techniques for doing it. They arrived in Europe with legal force in the EU's EIA Directive of 1985, and then in the World Bank's procedures for approving development projects and those of every other development bank and aid agency. The United Nations Rio Declaration of 1992 required every country to introduce Environmental Impact Assessment into national legislation and policy. By then similar techniques were being used to assess the social, health and other impacts of development projects, programmes, plans and policies. All these different types of impact often interact with each other, and almost always with impacts on the economy, so they were soon brought together within the framework of sustainable development. Variously described as integrated assessment, sustainability appraisal or sustainability impact assessment, all these initiatives drew on the principles that had been established in NEPA.

The European Commission's interest in applying the techniques to trade agreements led them to Norman Lee at Manchester University, who had chaired the EC's technical committee for developing the EIA Directive, and who was now working on integrated assessment with development economist Colin Kirkpatrick. The two of them joined forces with Oliver Morrissey, another development economist with extensive experience of international trade, to develop the SIA methodology (Kirkpatrick et al. 1999). At the time I was busy on an impact assessment programme for the World Bank and played only a minor role, to expand later as the EC's programme expanded.

In parallel similar approaches had been applied to the approval of all government legislation and policy. Again the USA had given the lead, with regulatory impact assessments that aimed to reduce the costs to businesses and the economy from unnecessary or badly designed laws and regulations. The UK and many other OECD countries introduced similar systems, followed by the EC for the development of all EU legislation and policy. Under the EC procedures that were introduced experimentally in 2002, to be issued in revised form in 2005, the scope of these assessments was expanded to cover all significant impacts. Known in the EU simply as Impact Assessment (IA), this procedural requirement might in principle replace the SIA studies when applied to trade policy. In practice the two types of study are carried out separately for different purposes. While a trade SIA contributes to the public dialogue on implementing a negotiating mandate, the IA contributes to developing the mandate and getting it approved by the Council of the European Union. Other IA studies conducted under the EC procedures are in the public domain. Those for trade policy are either very general and say almost nothing, or have to remain confidential in order to avoid revealing the EC's negotiating positions.

All these various applications and extensions of the impact assessment principles and techniques that were introduced in NEPA aim to ensure that decision-makers are provided with the best available evidence on the likely consequences of their decisions, and that they take them fully into account. What happens in practice is another matter.

DECISION-BASED EVIDENCE-MAKING

In countries with a free press governments cannot easily introduce a controversial policy without giving the public some kind of justification for it. The 'dodgy dossier' with which the British government launched the Iraq war is not a unique example of the kind of evidence that may be presented. The NEPA legislation aimed to curtail such practices for any government decision affecting the environment. It covered public policies, programmes and projects as well as private sector developments, but its initial application was mainly at the project level. The EU's EIA Directive applied only to development projects, and was not complemented by legislation covering plans and programmes until the Strategic Environmental Assessment Directive of 2001. Even this applied mainly to local government initiatives, and not to national policy or legislation. The EC's impact assessment procedures and similar systems in individual countries extend their requirements right up to the highest levels of public decision-making, but not without difficulty. Few government officials appreciate having their decisions subjected to external scrutiny. It can be forced on them by some higher authority, but they rarely volunteer for it. Cabinet ministers and EU Commissioners are no exception.

Ever since the introduction of NEPA and its derivatives academics have pored over the results to see whether they make any difference. Sometimes they do and sometimes they don't (Sadler 1996; Jacob et al. 2008; Ekins and Voituriez 2009). Most impact assessment systems make the proponents of development activities responsible for assessing the impacts of their own proposals, and for presenting their analysis in a report to the approval authority. Without exception every report argues that its proposal has been sufficiently well designed to be of great benefit with no significant adverse impacts. If the competent authority is sympathetic to the proposal it may accept the report without checking it very carefully. Most reviews of the quality of impact assessment reports reveal that in some cases their claims are valid while in others they are not, or the evidence presented is insufficient to justify the claims. This applies equally to private sector development projects, local government plans, and laws and policies introduced by government ministers or EU Commissioners. In many cases the impact assessment report fails to demonstrate that the decision has been based on the available evidence. Instead it presents carefully selected evidence in support of a decision that had already been made.[3]

The most important of the provisions to counter this that were introduced with NEPA, and retained in most other impact assessment systems, were its requirements for public involvement in the assessment process. When these are implemented effectively they can provide a valuable check on the competence of the competent authority. If the level of public interest in a proposal is low, the proponent may still be able to get away with unsubstantiated claims. When it is high those claims will be scrutinized by many interested observers, whose expertise in the relevant disciplines may be higher than that of the authors of the report and the officials responsible for checking it. Fear of being exposed to public ridicule can be a powerful incentive for doing the job properly.

This applies to the SIA studies of trade agreements as much as it does to any other assessment. In theory an impact assessment that is conducted by an independent organization should be less biased than one carried out by the proponent of the policy. In practice there is no such thing as an independent organization. In our case we were paid by the European Commission, and would not have had the chance to write more than one report if the Commission had taken great exception to it. Conversely, the whole SIA programme would have foundered if the civil society organizations at which it was aimed had seen it to be a worthless exercise. Irrespective of our own motives, we had little option but to evaluate both the EC's claims and the opposing counter-claims as thoroughly as we reasonably could. Note the word 'reasonably'. Careful examination of a typical SIA report will reveal that some of its messages are written on the lines while others are written between them.

THE SIA METHODOLOGY

Similar concerns to those which erupted at the WTO conference in Seattle had already been expressed during the negotiations on the North American Free Trade Agreement between Canada, Mexico and

---

BOX 3.1 THE DOHA AGENDA

Market access	Manufactured goods
	Agriculture
	Services
Singapore issues	Trade facilitation
	Government procurement
	Competition
	Investment
Other rules-based measures	Trade Related aspects of Intellectual Property Rights (TRIPs)
	Regional trade agreements
	Rules of origin
	Trade and environment
	Sanitary and phytosanitary measures
	Technical barriers to trade
	Subsidies, countervailing measures and anti-dumping
	Implementation issues in developing countries
	Dispute settlement
Other measures subject to discussion	Electronic commerce
	Trade, debt and finance
	Technical cooperation and capacity-building
	Technology transfer
	Special and differential treatment
	Least-developed countries
	Small economies

---

the USA. This led to the inclusion of an environmental chapter in the agreement and the creation by the three countries of their joint Council for Environmental Cooperation. The governments of the USA and Canada also introduced procedures for assessing the environmental impacts of other proposed trade agreements to which they were party. In developing the SIA methodology the Manchester team made full use of the North American work, along with other contributions from the OECD, UNEP's Economics and Trade Branch and international NGOs such as WWF, Friends of the Earth and Oxfam (George and Goldsmith 2006). Most of this work focused mainly on environmental impacts, in most cases with an emphasis on the host country. The methodology for the EC studies expanded on this to include economic and social impacts as well as environmental ones, in all the partner countries of a trade agreement as well as the one sponsoring the study.

The approach drew heavily on the experience accumulated since NEPA to incorporate a series of elements, which cover: consultation and stakeholder participation; screening the various components of an agreement to identify those whose impacts are likely to be significant; specifying the scope of the assessment; defining appropriate impact indicators; categorizing countries into groups with similar characteristics; analysing the baseline situation and expected changes; identifying one or more scenarios representing potential outcomes of the negotiations; assessing the likelihood and significance of impacts for those scenarios; evaluating alternative measures for enhancing beneficial impacts and avoiding or mitigating adverse ones; proposals for monitoring and evaluating the impacts of the implemented agreement (George and Kirkpatrick 2004).

Each study involves the publication of a series of reports, with consultation on each of these before proceeding to the next stage. A summary of the comments received is also published, along with a description of how they have been taken into account at each stage of the study. The assessment of potential impacts is the core of the analysis and is generally reported in at least two stages, giving opportunity for comment and critique before it is finalized.

The assessment needs to cover all the components of a trade negotiation agenda. As well as the elimination or reduction of tariffs and subsidies they include changes to a wide range of trade rules defined in WTO agreements, or variants of them in regional or bilateral agreements. The impacts of some of these can be as big as or bigger than those from removing tariffs. The main measures under negotiation in the WTO Doha agenda are given in Box 3.1. A regional or bilateral trade agreement may include the equivalents of any or all of these.

Most of the measures under discussion in the last group, and also some of the other rules-based measures in the third group, are directly related to the impacts of the other components of the negotiation agenda and were assessed in parallel with them. The rest were assessed separately in the studies for the WTO agenda, and similarly in any of the regional studies for which they were significant issues in the negotiations.

ASSESSING THE IMPACTS

The assessment generally begins by considering submissions from stakeholders, experts and other interested parties, on the basis of an inception report describing the methodology and proposed adaptations for the particular study. It then proceeds to assess each type of impact through a combination of theoretical analysis and empirical evidence from the research literature.

Most of the impacts are consequences of the economic effects. Two main types of effect are usually considered. Traditional trade theory concentrates on the *static equilibrium effects*, in which trade flows between countries change as a result of changes in prices or other incentives. In each of the countries affected production increases for some goods and services and decreases for others. For example, if Europe and America were to liberalize their agriculture their imports would go up, and their own agricultural production would go down. Capital and labour would move into manufactured goods and services, whose production would rise. The opposite would happen in those developing countries that export agricultural produce to Europe or America. Their production would go up in agriculture and down in other sectors, typically in manufacturing. These static equilibrium effects also lead to changes in overall economic efficiency, usually, though not always, increasing it.

Dynamic development effects occur when the rate of economic growth is accelerated or decelerated by changes in opportunities and incentives for social change and economic development. The shift of a developing country's resources into agricultural exports and out of manufacturing may reduce its rate of industrialization and its prospects of long-term growth. Both the static and the dynamic effects have economic, social and environmental impacts, differing between the short, medium and long term.

Two other effects are usually analysed. *Adjustment effects* occur during the period when trade flows and production levels are changing in response to the change in trade rules. With agricultural liberalization some farms go out of business and farm workers lose their jobs, while opportunities for both investment and employment increase in other sectors. It may take several years for capital and labour to move between sectors, with short-to-medium-term economic, social and environmental impacts. *Process effects* arise from changes in economic structure that may accelerate or decelerate existing processes of social transformation or environmental change. For example, increased incentives for agricultural exports may add to existing pressures and accelerate the rate of deforestation and loss of biodiversity.

The magnitude of the static equilibrium effects can be estimated using economic models, based mainly on computable general equilibrium analysis. These give an indication of the changes in trade flows and production levels, along with the overall effect on economic efficiency. They rarely attempt to model the dynamic nature of an economy, either in terms of its normal rate of growth and factors causing it, nor in terms of the process of adjustment. Instead they calculate the difference between two hypothetical equilibrium situations. The comparison does not model the actual mechanisms through which production falls in one sector and rises in another, nor the time taken for these changes to occur, nor any time difference between production decreases and increases. It provides only an indication of the size of the equilibrium changes, from which the SIA can assess the likely impacts during and after the process of adjustment.

Economic models are limited in what they are capable of modelling, and require many simplifying assumptions and approximations (Scrieciu 2007). This limits the accuracy and reliability of the findings. In principle it is quite easy to quantify the level of uncertainty in the numbers that come out, by obtaining a reliable measure for all those put in, adapting the algorithms to evaluate variances as well as mean values, defining the range of validity of each of the equations, and presenting a best estimate of uncertainty alongside each of the results. This is standard practice for any mathematical model whose misuse can have disastrous consequences that are traceable back to the modeller, such as in the design of a nuclear power station. It is rarely done for trade economics models. Scientific rigour tends to be unpopular with decision-makers, who generally use the studies to support their own proposals and may prefer not to know how far from the truth the results might be. A rough indication can be obtained from the spread of results from different studies. Plus or minus 50 per cent at a tolerable level of confidence is typical. In some cases the uncertainty is bigger than the number itself, such that a number predicted to be positive could easily be negative. When the equations in the models are used outside their range of validity the numbers become meaningless. Considerable care is needed in interpreting the results.

The modelling of services trade is even less reliable than for industrial and agricultural goods. Data are limited, and the barriers are generally qualitative and have to be converted into quantitative equivalents. The same applies to all the other components of a negotiation agenda. None of these can be modelled with any great confidence, if at all. Some models go beyond equilibrium calculations to estimate some of the dynamic effects, but the assumptions and approximations involved are even greater than for equilibrium analysis. For assessing dynamic effects the SIA studies have generally relied on qualitative considerations and empirical evidence from past experience.

The results from the models are used in conjunction with a broader analysis of cause-and-effect relationships for each component of the negotiation agenda, drawing on the available research literature. Social impacts caused by the economic effects include changes in unemployment levels as production moves between sectors, influences on wage rates for different types of work, differential gender effects, external and internal migration (particularly between rural and urban areas), and others associated with changes in government revenue and expenditure. All of these can be significant during the adjustment period, and also subsequently if domestic policies are inadequate for responding to the changes. Environmental impacts are assessed using similar techniques to those employed in environmental assessments. They include the knock-on effects of population movements and changes in land use, as well as the direct impacts of the production changes. In cases where there is limited theoretical knowledge or empirical evidence of the effects of past episodes of trade liberalization, much of the analysis consists of evaluating the validity of the various claims made by negotiating parties and other stakeholders.

The assessment of impacts should always conclude with an evaluation of their likely significance. This is a key aspect of the methodology inherited from NEPA. It typically entails comparing the predicted impact with the baseline situation and existing trends, and can be particularly valuable when evaluating the various claims. It is often argued that a proposal offers huge benefits because it is worth many billions of dollars. When compared with the size of the economy and its normal rate of growth these enormous numbers can fade into insignificance.

INTERPRETING THE EVIDENCE

None of the evidence on the impacts of trade liberalization is entirely conclusive. Theories abound, some complementing each other and others conflicting with each other. Every effect observed in the past has multiple causes, some directly associated with trade and some not. It is rarely possible to fully disentangle what was due to what. In predicting the likely consequences of a proposed trade agreement the assessor has to make his or her own best judgement from the evidence available.

The judgements presented in the rest of the book are those of the author alone, based on the evidence as described. Much of this comes from the SIA reports and the sources they used, along with other more recent information. Many of the conclusions are broadly the same as those of the corresponding SIA studies, whether the author was directly involved in them or not. Others are strictly the author's own interpretation. Most are stated less circumspectly than in the reports.

In the speech quoted at the beginning of Chapter 2, Europe's Trade Commissioner, Peter Mandelson, acknowledged that the short-term pain of trade liberalization can be acute, and may not be balanced by any long-term gain. He observed that it might not even lead to greater economic growth, let alone to poverty reduction or environmental sustainability. It was a blunt statement. The evidence suggests that it was not blunt enough.

TWO | IMPACTS

INTRODUCTION

According to traditional trade economics theory the removal of barriers to free trade results in an increase in economic efficiency from which all countries should gain economically. This gain can then be distributed in such a way that everyone in every country should benefit, and should be available for improving the quality of the natural environment as well. The theory accepts that there may be some adverse effects as each country's economy adjusts to the new conditions, but in the end everybody is expected to be a winner, and the quality of the environment should also improve.

What happens in practice depends on many complex factors. Chapter 4 examines the actual impacts of removing barriers to trade in manufactured goods. Chapter 5 examines those of liberalizing agricultural trade, including the removal of both import taxes and subsidies. The liberalization of trade in services is examined in Chapter 6, covering all the different types of services. Chapters 7, 8 and 9 cover the rules that form the remainder of the negotiation agenda. The impact of rules on Trade-Related aspects of Intellectual Property Rights (TRIPs) is examined in Chapter 7. Chapter 8 examines the impacts of four other components of the negotiation agenda that are collectively known as the Singapore issues: trade facilitation, government procurement, competition policy and investment. Chapter 9 examines the various rules that comprise the other main components of the agenda. It concludes with one additional item, trade in oil and other mineral resources. This is not on the liberalization agenda, as there are few trade barriers to be removed, but the impact on sustainable development can be among the biggest of all.

4 | CLIMBING THE DEVELOPMENT LADDER

Under George I English statesmen had long ago clearly perceived the grounds on which the greatness of the nation depends. At the opening of Parliament in 1721, the King is made to say by the Ministry that 'it is evident that nothing so much contributes to promote the public well-being as the exportation of manufactured goods and the importation of foreign raw material'. (List 1885 [1841]: 50)

When Britain was the only industrial power it exported its manufactured goods in return for imports of foreign raw material. Following the advice of Friedrich List, Germany developed the ability to do the same, as did the rest of Europe and North America. Japan followed suit, and then the newly industrializing countries of South-East Asia and now China. Many other developing countries have been left behind. They still export their raw materials, and still import most of their manufactured goods.

In this chapter we examine the extent to which the further liberalization of manufacturing trade would change that situation, and the consequent effects on development, environment and people. We find that the ability of the industrialized and newly industrializing countries to wage trade wars with each other would be reduced, and costs come down through the economies of scale of global markets. Wages go up in some of the larger and more advanced developing countries, including China. In many others wage rates go down and unemployment goes up. The countries that have had the least success in industrial development find it even harder. Many of the poorest countries experience a significant loss of government revenue, with a strong likelihood of expenditure cuts in health, education, environmental protection and social support. In China and other countries where manufacturing production goes up, pollution rises from levels that are already high. The effects on climate change are small, but go in the wrong direction.

TRADE IN MANUFACTURED GOODS

The consumption of goods made in foreign countries is now commonplace. In both industrial countries and developing ones many consumer goods are imported, as are motor vehicles and other high-value products.

Brand names have become global, with little indication of where the products are made, or even of whether the company that owns the brand is based at home or abroad. Buying products that are made anywhere in the global economy has become the norm, yet it still raises many concerns. Does it weaken our own economy or strengthen it? Does it help the economic development of poorer countries or hinder it? Does it destroy jobs in our own country or stimulate the creation of new ones that are more interesting and better paid? Does it exploit poorly paid workers in the countries that make the goods, or does it create jobs for people who would otherwise be unemployed? Does shipping goods around the world damage the environment, or does it enable efficiencies that help to conserve the environment? Does a trade agreement that aims to raise the level of imports and exports even higher make the bad things worse, or make the good ones better?

The answers presented in this chapter come mainly from the series of impact assessment studies that were carried out for the Doha agenda of the WTO negotiations,[4] along with some of the findings of the regional studies. The Doha assessments began in 2002, shortly after the Doha ministerial meeting, with a preliminary overview SIA of the whole agenda. They continued with detailed assessments of particular agenda components, and concluded in 2006 with a final overview study. This drew together the findings of the other studies and updated them for the minimal progress made at the ministerial meeting in Hong Kong at the end of 2005.

These studies examined the impacts of the trade liberalization agenda for non-agricultural market access, the jargon for reducing barriers to trade in manufactured goods.

TRADITIONAL ECONOMIC GAINS FROM LIBERALIZING TRADE IN MANUFACTURES

The advent of sophisticated computer modelling techniques has made it possible to estimate the magnitude of the economic benefit that has traditionally been expected from trade liberalization. Taking account of the uncertainties, the modelling studies that we reviewed confirmed that the net effect on the global economy is likely to be positive, but small. For some countries the effect could be negative, but also small. The overall results indicate that full liberalization of both manufactured and agricultural goods (removing all tariffs and agricultural subsidies) would give a rise in global economic welfare of about US$125 billion. The contribution from eliminating tariffs on manufactured goods would be about $45 billion. For the smaller tariff reductions envisaged in the actual Doha negotiations, this would come down to about $15 billion. As a percentage of the total size of the global economy these numbers are small. Compared with the rise in welfare expected from other sources they are vanishingly small.

Trade officials whose policies rely on David Ricardo's theory of comparative advantage have found this hard to believe. In one of our meetings with Europe's trade negotiators the chief official kept his counsel while we debated the point with his junior colleagues. The welfare increase being predicted at the time was about half a per cent of global GDP, which, they insisted, would amount to much more than that, since the extra half a per cent would be received every year for ever. That may be true, but the increase is still only half a per cent. If I were offered an annual wage rise of half a per cent I would not be very happy. If I were told that it was the only rise I would get for the next ten years I would be ten times less happy. If I were then told that it would be phased in over those ten years, so that my accumulating knowledge and experience would be rewarded with a rise of just one twentieth of a per cent each year, I might regard it as something of an insult.

Even highly respected economists have found it hard to accept that Ricardo's theory produces such small numbers. They have made the same mistake in interpreting them. At a gathering of leading economic modellers that we attended at WTO headquarters in Geneva, one of the invited speakers presented an otherwise excellent paper that exaggerated the importance of the increase in world income due to tariff removal by referring to it as a rate of change, implying that income would increase by that amount each year. It does not. It is not a rate of change, it is a single one-off change, giving a single one-off rise in income. When the error was pointed out he immediately agreed that it was a mistake. It is an understandable mistake. The assumption that comparative advantage offers big gains has been a major component of orthodox economic theory for nearly two centuries.

Other economists who are quite sceptical about the benefits of free trade have made the same mistake, by suggesting that the welfare gains to developing countries estimated by their model would make a moderately useful contribution to poverty reduction because it represents an addition of 0.1 per cent to GDP growth each year. It does not. It adds 0.1 per cent to GDP, once only, equivalent to just one year's growth of that amount. When the article was subsequently republished in a United Nations book the authors corrected the error. They still argued, however, that the gain was worth much more because it would grow at compound interest to become ten times as much in ten years' time.

If that were true the same would also apply to the other 99.9 per cent. That too would grow by a factor of ten, to leave the effect of trade liberalization still no more than a tenth of a per cent. The argument is the equivalent of assuming that the extra amount, and only that amount, is invested in a bank. It is not. It is spent, on the food that we eat and everything else that comprises GDP. The confusion arises from treating the world's income and expenditure account as if it were a balance sheet. Economists are not accountants. The subject generally features in their education to about the same extent as evolutionary biology, social anthropology and atmospheric physics. Those who have yet to explore it might do well to take a lesson in accountancy from the proprietor of their local corner shop.

American economists Mark Weisbrot and Dean Baker have been pointing out for years that the many billions of dollars a year efficiency gains that come from trade liberalization are worth very little when compared with the size of the global economy and its normal rate of growth (Weisbrot and Baker 2005). We followed their lead to make the same comparison. At the time the calculations were done the size of the global economy was a little over $27,000 billion a year, measured as the total of Net National Income. The estimated welfare gain of $45 billion that would come from completely removing all tariffs on manufactured goods is about 0.17 per cent of that. It would take well over ten years to achieve it, from the end of the previous round of negotiations to the eventual implementation of a new agreement. At its normal growth rate of over 3 per cent a year the world economy would grow in that time by well over 30 per cent. Even if all tariffs and subsidies were completely removed it would take more than ten years to get a gain of 0.17 per cent, compared with over 30 per cent occurring by other means. The conventional economic welfare benefit of fully liberalizing trade in manufactured goods is barely one two hundredth of what can usually be expected from other sources. For the more limited liberalization of the Doha negotiations the gain would be three times smaller still, less than one five hundredth of the effect of normal economic growth.

This does not mean that trade is unimportant for development. It can be hugely beneficial or hugely detrimental, depending on how it is organized. These big gains or losses come from the dynamic effects, however, not the static ones. Whether they are beneficial or adverse depends strongly on whether a country uses trade as part of a carefully designed development strategy or just lets it happen. Either way they can have a far more significant impact on economic welfare than the static efficiency effects that have traditionally been expected from the theory of comparative advantage. Before examining the dynamic effects we will take a look at the price that has to be paid for achieving the minimal efficiency gains.

LOSS OF GOVERNMENT REVENUES

The most immediate impact of reducing tariffs is a loss of government revenue. This is no problem in high-income countries, where most tax is raised from other sources. Nor is it a problem in developing countries that are rich in oil or other minerals, which get most of their government income from selling them. In many other developing countries import taxes are a much bigger proportion of government revenue. Any reduction of tariffs will reduce that revenue. There have been cases when liberalization has increased the volume of imports so much that receipts have risen despite the lower tax rate. Such cases are rare, and have been accompanied by a rapidly rising trade deficit and serious exchange rate difficulties. In general the net effect on government revenue is negative. Unless the same amount of tax is levied by other means, government expenditure has to be cut. In countries that are highly dependent on import taxes this would put pressure on all areas of the budget, with potentially significant adverse impacts on health, education, social support programmes and environmental protection. If some other tax is used to replace the lost revenue, it may tax the rich less than before and the poor more.

Some of the least developed countries (LDCs) obtain more than half their government income from tariff revenues. The average for all LDCs is about a third (Laird et al. 2006). The agenda agreed in Doha did not require these countries to reduce their applied tariff rates, and so there would be no immediate impact. The agenda did, however, require that they reduce their bound tariffs (the maximum that can be applied) to the level of their current applied rates. This would reduce their flexibility to adjust tariffs to maintain revenue when the mix of products they import changes.

Other developing countries are required to reduce their applied tariffs and will therefore experience an immediate impact on revenue. On average tariffs contribute about 14 per cent of total revenue in these countries. The proportion is about 10 per cent in China, 18 per cent in India and over 25 per cent in many of the smaller countries (ibid.; Kowalski 2005). Without a rise in other taxes full tariff removal would reduce government income by roughly those amounts. Even with less ambitious liberalization the impact can still be highly significant. For the least ambitious of the Doha proposals the estimated loss of government revenue in sub-Saharan

Africa averages about 2 per cent. It rises to nearly 10 per cent for the most ambitious proposals, which still fell well short of full liberalization. The impact is similar in India, while in North Africa it ranges from 4 per cent for the least ambitious proposals up to 20 per cent for the most ambitious. All of these estimates are for liberalizing both agricultural and manufactured goods. The biggest effect comes from manufactures, for which it is typically about three-quarters of the total.

According to IMF data trade liberalization has been associated with a marked decline in trade tax revenue for the past twenty years (IMF 2005). In middle-income countries tariff income as a share of GDP fell by about a third, while in low-income ones the decline was over 40 per cent. Most middle-income countries have increased other taxes in response and their total revenues have remained broadly unchanged. This is not the case in low-income countries, which have found it much harder to generate income from other sources. Their total government revenue has declined in parallel with the falling tariff revenue, by about 40 per cent. As the IMF observes, the consequent cuts in government expenditure have made it even harder for these countries to provide social support for the workers who are displaced by the trade reforms.

Even if all the lost revenue is replaced by other taxes there can still be significant adverse effects. A detailed study of the Philippines for the World Bank estimated that a compensatory indirect tax would reduce the incidence of poverty marginally, but would substantially increase its severity (Cororaton et al. 2006). The same study showed that if an income tax is used instead the severity of poverty increases even more, and its incidence goes up as well. A similar study for Cameroon examined three different ways of replacing the lost revenue. If a neutral tax were used the poverty headcount index would increase from 40.2 per cent to 40.8 per cent. With VAT the rise would be three times bigger, and five times bigger with a consumption tax (Emini et al. 2006).

In theory it is possible to implement a package of tax reforms that would replace the lost revenues without increasing poverty. In practice it has not always been done, particularly in the poorest countries. The reforms are often opposed by powerful interest groups and are not implemented. Even when they are they need to be very carefully designed if they are to have the desired effect.

PRODUCTION EFFECTS

The changes that are expected in economic welfare occur because, in David Ricardo's terms, it should be more efficient to produce wine in France, corn in America and manufactured goods in England. To get the expected economic benefit, however big or small, America would have to shut down all its factories, abandon all its vineyards and devote itself to growing corn. America's comparative advantages have changed since Ricardo's time but the principle is the same. When trade barriers are removed every country produces less of some things and more of others, and makes up the difference in imports and exports. The net effect on economic efficiency and welfare may be small, but the production changes that are needed to achieve it can be big.

Some of the economic modelling studies that we reviewed were particularly useful for assessing the impacts because they gave production information as well as the net effect on economic welfare. We used this information to estimate the magnitude of the changes in manufacturing production that would occur from full liberalization of trade in goods, with all tariffs and agricultural subsidies removed.[5]

The changes were estimated for all economic sectors in all parts of the world, consolidated into fifteen product groups and twenty-four countries or country groups. Of the 360 results, 115 show an increase or decrease in production of 5 per cent or more. In sixty-four cases the change in production is over 10 per cent. In twenty-one cases production rises or falls by more than 20 per cent. Many of the numbers are averages for a group of countries and will be larger for individual ones. All the numbers are averages for a whole economic sector, and mask the effects of higher tariffs on individual types of product (tariff peaks). For these products, which are the most politically sensitive and the most highly protected from foreign competition, the production changes may be much bigger than the average values. All the numbers could be bigger still, or smaller, because of the uncertainties arising from assumptions and approximations inherent in economic modelling. The changes experienced in practice could easily differ from the estimates by well over a factor of two in either direction.[6]

The production of clothing in India is estimated to go up by nearly 40 per cent, by nearly 30 per cent in Indonesia and over 20 per cent in China. What some countries gain others lose. Clothing production is estimated to fall by 11 per cent in the old member states of the European Union, by 20 per cent in the new member states, by 15 per cent in the USA, by 22 per cent in other OECD countries, by 18 per cent in Mexico and by 25 per cent in the Middle East and North Africa. Leather goods and footwear show similarly large declines in these countries, as well as in Bangladesh, where production falls by 22 per cent. Production of electronic equipment goes up by 10 per cent in Mexico and down by more than 10 per cent in most of the rest of Latin America.

Bangladesh and some of the other least developed countries are among the biggest losers. Under WTO rules these countries can be given preferential treatment for their exports, and lose that advantage when the barriers to other countries' exports are removed as well. In sub-Saharan Africa the effects are almost universally negative. Except in South Africa, production falls across nearly the whole of manufacturing industry.

These numbers are no more than rough estimates of the size of the effects, as indicated by the same economic models that are used to show how big the welfare gains would be. Compared with the size of the economy and its normal rate of growth, the welfare gains are small. The production changes needed to achieve them are big. The numbers estimated above are for full liberalization, and the effects of any likely conclusion to the Doha Round would be smaller. The welfare effects would also be smaller. The ambitions of the round have shrunk, not because of any concern for the adverse impacts, but because Europe's and America's trade negotiators have failed to achieve what they aimed to achieve in Seattle.

EMPLOYMENT

Where production goes up employment goes up, and vice versa. Trade liberalization can also help to increase productivity, which makes the positive employment effects smaller and the negative ones bigger. With that proviso the percentage changes in employment will be similar to those for production.

Most general equilibrium economic models assume full employment, and so cannot calculate the net effect on overall employment levels. It is possible to adjust the equations to give a result, but the analysis is so far removed from reality that it is not worth doing. Models that attempt to do it calculate an expected outcome once the global economy has adjusted to the change in trade rules, as though the change occurred instantaneously. The analysis takes no account of what happens while the economy is adjusting from one pseudo-equilibrium to another, which takes several years. The best that can be done at all reliably is to get a rough estimate of how much employment might go up in one economic sector, and an equally rough estimate of how much it might go down in another. If all manufacturing sectors go in one direction and all agricultural sectors go in the opposite direction, we can get a reasonable estimate of the overall effect for each. The level of uncertainty is far too high to give any reliable indication of whether increases and decreases cancel each other out. For that we have to use a more qualitative analysis of the dynamic effects.

The process of adjustment begins with rising production in countries and sectors where firms are able to take immediate advantage of the new opportunities, which typically occurs where firms are large and the new exports are a small proportion of their output. Production falls in the same sectors in the importing countries. There may be a significant time lag before new jobs appear in other sectors, since the resources needed for their expansion may not be readily available. New capital investment may be needed, new facilities may have to be built, new products may have to be developed to satisfy other countries' standards or consumer preferences, workers may need to move from one part of the country to another, and they may have to learn completely new skills. In some countries newly competitive economic sectors will expand and suck labour from less competitive ones. In other countries newly uncompetitive sectors will contract and release labour for which no new employment has yet become available. In many countries, particularly small ones, the time lags result in a higher overall level of unemployment throughout the period of adjustment. In some of the poorest, particularly in sub-Saharan Africa, severe supply-side constraints in the domestic economy make the problem worse. The new capital, the new facilities, the newly designed products and the newly trained, newly relocated people that are assumed to take up the slack may never materialize. In those countries overall unemployment goes up and stays up.

For most industrial countries the calculations indicate that employment will decrease significantly in textiles, clothing, leather goods and footwear. This is a continuation of previous trends, in which employment has declined in these sectors and risen in service industries. In these countries overall unemployment levels are expected to stay fairly constant, with former textile workers joining the pool of unemployed and others leaving it to work in services.

Impacts in developing countries vary according to their present levels of unemployment and the different ways in which their economies are evolving. In India, China and several other Asian countries employment would rise significantly in textiles, clothing and footwear. Here too this continues previous trends. In China rising demand for unskilled labour in manufacturing has led to low urban unemployment and extensive migration from rural areas to the cities. The additional demand for labour would have to be met by further migration. In India urban unemployment is higher, at around 9 per cent.[7] The increase in production would help to reduce it, and the effect on migration would be smaller than in China. In Bangladesh urban unemployment is already over 25 per cent and would become even higher from the decline in manufacturing production.

Similar problems are identified in the Middle East and North Africa, Argentina and much of the rest of Latin America. Manufacturing employment goes down, particularly in the textile, clothing and footwear sectors, with urban unemployment already high. Mexico is an exception, with a fall in production in these sectors, but relatively low current levels of urban unemployment.

In the whole of sub-Saharan Africa the projected impacts on manufacturing employment are significantly adverse. Even in South Africa, where production goes up in some sectors, declining demand for low-skill labour can be expected to aggravate an urban unskilled unemployment level of over 20 per cent. In the rest of sub-Saharan Africa urban unemployment is nearly as high, and the demand for labour is projected to shrink in almost every industrial sector.

WAGE LEVELS, WORKING CONDITIONS AND GENDER EFFECTS

The changes in employment have a knock-on effect on wage rates. Equilibrium economic models can be used to calculate the size of the effects, but the results are as meaningless as those for the overall level of unemployment, for the same reasons. Again a more reliable indication comes from qualitative analysis of the effects.

In sectors where production declines, downward pressure on wages can be expected. In sectors where it rises the effect on wage rates is mainly positive, but will depend on the level of unemployment in the cities and on the changes taking place in the countryside. In China, where urban unemployment is low and additional manufacturing labour has to be attracted from rural areas, wage rates are likely to continue rising. Most of the reduction in global poverty that has occurred in the past few decades has been due to rising wage rates in China (World Bank 2003a). In countries where urban unemployment is higher an increase in manufacturing production may not lead to any increase in wages. This will apply particularly in those countries where rural–urban migration is driven by shrinking livelihood opportunities in rural areas. In countries where job losses occur before new ones are created there will be a net adverse effect on employment throughout the adjustment period, with a consequent fall in wage rates.

The effects on working conditions are closely related to movements in employment between the informal and formal sectors of manufacturing production. Core labour standards tend to be significantly better in internationally managed export industries than in domestic firms, but extensive subcontracting takes place. The textile and clothing sector is the most affected by trade liberalization, and predominantly employs low-skill, low-income workers. The sector generally has a high proportion of female labour, with concerns over the use of child labour in some countries. The creation of export processing zones presents particular problems. Trade unions have persistently documented violations of core labour standards in many of these zones (ICFTU 2002, 2003; Sengenberger 2005). The ILO's World Commission on the Social Dimension of Globalization has identified many problems in such zones, including low wages, intimidation of workers trying to join or form trade unions, violence, exploitation of women workers and sexual harassment, all of which show evidence of having expanded dramatically (WCSDG 2004).

A United Nations review of the relationship between trade and development has concluded that women have been incorporated into paid employment in greater numbers than men, but usually under inferior conditions (United Nations 1999). The costs of economic adjustment have been borne disproportionately by women, especially poor women, and women have experienced the biggest effects of reductions in social expenditure. Other studies have indicated that net job creation may be significantly higher for women than for men, mainly through deskilling and increased flexibility, but with significantly higher job uncertainty (Ozler et al. 2004). Research in India shows that there has been an increase in women's employment, particularly in the clothing sector, but no simultaneous improvement in their working conditions or wages (Jha 2006). The study raises the question of what the newly employed women were doing before. When traditional rural livelihoods disappear through the commercialization and mechanization of agriculture, even the worst of wages and working conditions in the city may become the only option available.

Adverse gender impacts may also occur in high-income countries. It has been observed that in industries where international competition is strong, women and ethnic minorities tend to represent a significantly larger share of job losers (OECD 2005).

Consumer pressure in the EU, the USA and other developed countries has encouraged international corporations to address these issues, along with governments' encouragement of companies to pursue policies of Corporate Social Responsibility (European Commission 2001b, 2002a). Difficulties remain in applying labour standards beyond the major companies to their subcontracting chains. Many concerns have been expressed about employment and working conditions in both formal and informal enterprises (WCSDG 2004). In India it has been estimated that only 7 per cent of workers are in the organized sector, with the rest working on casual contracts in large or small firms or in household production. These activities are only partly covered by labour laws (Harris-White 2003). The ILO's report concludes that global markets have grown rapidly without the parallel development of suitable economic and social institutions (WCSDG 2004). It argues for stronger action to develop such institutions, for export processing zones in particular and for global production systems in general.

All of these effects on wages and working conditions occur in the short to medium term. In the longer term the impacts depend on whether trade liberalization helps or hinders the dynamic process of transforming countries' economies towards higher employment levels, higher skill levels and higher-added-value work. We will look at these dynamic effects after we have explored the environmental ones.

ENVIRONMENTAL IMPACTS

In parallel with the main negotiations on reducing or removing trade barriers the WTO negotiates separate agreements on trade and environment. These cover special provisions for trade in environmental goods as well as other environment-related measures, which we examine in Chapter 9, along with other WTO rules. The main environmental impacts of trade liberalization come from the main negotiations.

Manufacturing liberalization has two main types of impact on climate change, alongside others arising from other aspects of the negotiation agenda. One is associated with transport and the other with the movements in production. The amount of greenhouse gas generated in the manufacture of a product varies between countries, so that total emissions will increase or decrease when production moves from one country to another. For one of the regional trade agreements estimates based on economic modelling indicated that this effect would reduce the region's carbon emissions by about a tenth of a per cent (IARC 2007a). For global trade liberalization the effect could be in either direction but is likely to be similar in size and too small to be significant. The increase in emissions due to increased transport is bigger, but is still a small proportion of total global emissions. We estimated that the transport effect of full trade liberalization would increase total global greenhouse gas emissions by about half a per cent.[8] This would accelerate climate change rather than helping to slow it, but the size of the effect is small compared with the size of the problem.

Some of the other potential impacts are also fairly small. Concerns have been expressed that trade liberalization might encourage polluting industries to relocate to developing countries, where regulation is often weaker. Most studies of this 'pollution haven' thesis suggest that many of the concerns are unwarranted. High-technology international corporations typically introduce manufacturing techniques and management systems that are more environmentally friendly than those of their domestic competitors (Grossman 2002; van Liemt 2001; UNEP/IISD 2005). This in turn tends to stimulate the introduction of such technologies in domestic companies, since environmentally efficient technologies are often more economically competitive. Recent studies have identified significant pollution haven effects for some industries, such as in the extraction of copper and other polluting materials (UNEP/IISD 2005), but not as a general effect (Brunnermeier and Levinson 2004). The environmental impacts of manufacturing are strongly dependent on the nature of the industry and the effectiveness of the domestic regulatory framework (Kirkpatrick et al. 2004; Kirkpatrick and Watanabe 2006).

In industries where local supply chains using small and dirty cottage industries remain economically viable, trade liberalization has little effect on pollution intensity. In industries where production costs favour consolidation into fewer, larger units, the ability to control polluting emissions tends to be enhanced and gives regulators the opportunity to set and enforce stricter standards. If full transfer of technologies and skills were to take place it would prevent an overall global increase in pollution when production moves between countries. Even this, however, would not reduce the main environmental impacts of reducing trade barriers for manufactured goods. Whatever the relative levels of technology and regulation, the pollution moves with the production. The impacts decrease in countries where production falls and increase where it rises. The changes do not cancel each other out. Except for global impacts such as carbon emissions, reduced environmental damage in one country does not compensate for rising damage in another.

Measured in dollar values the biggest movements of production are in the textile and clothing industry. The environmental impacts of the industry are spread throughout the product life-cycle, with different issues arising in fibre production, processing, spinning, yarn preparation, fabric production, bleaching, dyeing, printing, finishing, use and disposal. The main water pollution comes from the use of solvents and pesticides in processing raw wool and cotton, and the use of dyes and bleaches at later stages. All of these pollutants may be discharged into waste water, and need proper treatment to avoid significant downstream damage to the natural environment and to other water users. There may also be significant local impacts on water resources in areas where these are limited or needed by other users. The production of dyes and pigments produces significant pollutants in air as well as water. Air emissions from textile production include dust, oil mists, acid vapours and the nitrogen and sulphur oxides in boiler exhausts. Solid waste in the form of sludges often contains toxic organic chemicals and metals.

All other sectors of manufacturing industry generate air pollution, water pollution and solid wastes in varying degrees, along with the consumption of water and other resources. The impacts will increase or decrease in individual countries in approximate proportion to the production changes, offset only partly by the expected improvements in technology and regulation.

Many developing countries already suffer from high levels of pollution and declining supplies of water and other resources. In absolute terms the largest production increases occur in China. China has a much stronger regulatory regime than many other developing countries and has made considerable progress in strengthening it further. The OECD warns that these efforts have not kept pace with the environmental pressures created by the country's rapid economic growth (OECD 2006). Air quality in some Chinese cities is among the worst in the world. Many watercourses, lakes and coastal waters are severely polluted and present a major threat to human health. Of the country's 600 largest cities, 400 suffer from water shortages. In many areas the abstraction of groundwater far exceeds the replenishment rate. Industrial waste and hazardous waste are produced faster than the capacity of disposal systems to absorb them, and are stored awaiting treatment or tipped on proliferating uncontrolled dumps. All of these problems are caused, at least in part, and in some cases entirely, by industries whose production levels would rise even higher through the proposed trade liberalization measures.

These problems are not unique to China. The faster production grows, the harder it is for environmental regulation to keep pace with it. In most of the developing countries for which trade liberalization leads to a significant increase in production, significant environmental problems become significantly worse.

DYNAMIC EFFECTS

The transfers of production from one country to another that result from removing tariffs and other trade barriers represent a one-off rearrangement of each country's economy as it adjusts to a change in trade rules. This change is superimposed on many other factors in a country's development. The high rates of growth in China, India and some other developing countries are due primarily to dynamic processes of structural transformation within these countries' own economies. If a change in trade rules accelerates or decelerates these dynamic processes, the consequent change in growth rates can have a far greater long-term impact on economic welfare than the minimal efficiency gains.

Having discovered that the static effects are smaller than they expected, some economic modellers have turned their attention to the dynamic ones. The results can be misleading. Some of the effects can be modelled reasonably reliably but the biggest ones cannot. They depend on specific decisions made by governments, which do not obey any mathematical formula. If a government decides to adopt a neoliberal economic policy of minimum interference in the market, the consequences will be very different from those of an interventionist approach. Different forms of intervention will have different effects, as will specific aspects of each. Government decisions on such matters are no more readily predicted by the numbers in an equation than those of an individual person or a company. A mathematical model can forecast the aggregate consequences of decisions made by a thousand competing entrepreneurs tolerably well. It cannot predict the individual consequences for each, which differ dramatically according to who succeeds in outcompeting whom.

Although the overall efficiency gains that come from liberalizing trade in manufactured goods are much smaller than originally expected, much larger gains come from economies of scale. These accrue only to those countries whose firms have the technologies and skills to compete in global markets. Restrictive trade rules that commit high-income countries to opening their borders and keeping them open enable them to tap these gains while protecting them from trade wars with each other. Applying the same rules to countries that do not yet have the ability to compete protects the global haves from the global have-nots (Reinert 2007).

The efficiency gains expected from trade liberalization result from every country concentrating on producing those goods or services in which it has a comparative advantage. The comparative advantages of high-income countries are in high-added-value products and services, such as communication systems and financial services, with high technology content and high skill levels. Those of low-income countries are in low-wage products and commodities, such as clothing, minerals and agricultural produce. For a country to develop economically and socially it has to change those comparative advantages. Trade rules that reinforce the existing ones make the task considerably harder.

Countries with relatively low trade barriers tend to have relatively high rates of economic growth. Some economists have taken this as proof of the neoliberal theory that reducing the barriers increases the growth (Dollar and Kraay 2000, 2004). Others point out that the observation provides no evidence of cause and effect. The statement is just as true the other way round, that countries with high growth rates tend to have low trade barriers. As Friedrich List pointed out in the nineteenth century, Britain protected its industry and commerce from foreign competition until it was well on the way to achieving global dominance. The rest of Europe, America, Japan and the newly industrializing countries of East Asia all did much the same until their manufacturing industries were strong enough to compete internationally (Chang 2002). Most of the trade liberalization measures in South Korea and Taiwan were introduced in the 1980s, two decades after they had embarked on their dramatic transformations towards becoming fully developed industrial economies (Rodrik 2001). The smaller 'tiger' economies of Singapore and Hong Kong used similarly interventionist policies in the early stages of their development (Pangestu 2002; UNIDO 2002).

Neoliberal theory argues that these policies were counterproductive, and that governments should instead rely on generic policy measures to create an economic environment conducive to investment, innovation and competition (Pangestu 2002). This flies in the face of history. Neither the industrialized countries nor the newly industrializing ones that are now joining them relied on generic policy measures to achieve their goals (Amsden 1997). All used a wide variety of trade-distorting measures to protect and promote their manufacturing industries until they were internationally competitive. Korea, Taiwan and the other newly industrializing countries of East Asia protected their domestic markets with high tariffs, provided large subsidies for exports, encouraged firms to circumvent other countries' patents, and subjected foreign investors to limitations on their ownership of domestic companies and a minimum level of domestic content in their production (Rodrik 2001; Lall and Theubal 1998). Such measures are now severely restricted by WTO rules, and even more in many bilateral agreements (Thrasher and Gallagher 2008). Full trade liberalization would prohibit them completely, other than for limited exemptions through provisions for special and differential treatment. These apply mainly to the least developed countries, whose manufacturing industries are too weak to pose any kind of threat to the developed ones.

The protection of domestic industry through high tariffs and other trade barriers would not, on its own, accelerate industrial development in the least developed countries and other low-income ones. The East

Asian success involved many other factors, differing between countries according to their particular circumstances, and integrating urban development with rural development (see Box 4.1). The freedom to define their own trade policy was a necessary condition for their development but not a sufficient one.

A country cannot develop by isolating itself from international trade. Nor can it do so by allowing itself to be restricted to exporting low-added-value products and importing high-added-value ones. If it attempts to produce the high-added-value ones itself through an import substitution strategy in which it makes them only for its own market it will never achieve the economies of scale that are needed for international competitiveness. It has to attack the global market, in the face of large and powerful competitors that are already well established. This has typically entailed targeting specific industries, providing incentives for capital investment in those industries, investing in research and development in their particular sciences and technologies, and setting up education and training programmes tailored to their specific needs (Choi 1986). Picking winners is not the impossibility that is often claimed. Governments have proved perfectly capable of it, provided that they work closely with the private sector, research the options thoroughly, and pick enough potential winners to allow for some of them to lose (Hausmann, Pritchett and Rodrik 2004; Hausmann, Rodrik and Velasco 2004; Helpman 2004; Romer 1986; Wade 2003).

The textile and clothing industry might be a winner for some countries, such as Vietnam. For most others it can only be in niche markets. Now that China and other large countries with low labour costs have obtained the necessary technologies and skills, the opportunities for other countries to compete effectively are severely limited. Much the same applies to every manufacturing sector. When Korean institutions did their research into which sectors might lead the country's industrial expansion they found that the range of realistic options was extremely small (Choi 1986). Countries that aim to follow Korea's example need to do their own research just as thoroughly. They are not helped by international policies that discourage them from doing it at all, and trade rules that prevent them from acting on the results.

Since the confrontations at the 1999 Seattle WTO conference the larger developing countries have exercised considerable influence in the negotiations. Smaller countries often face a choice between accepting what they are offered and losing what they have already got. China, India and Brazil are not in that position. Their markets are big enough to give them the power to block any negotiated agreement that is not to their

BOX 4.1 THE EVOLUTION OF KOREA'S DEVELOPMENT STRATEGY

First five-year plan (1962–66)
- initial focus on light, labour-intensive industries
- intention to change the economy from labour intensive to technology intensive
- export orientation in parallel with import substitution
- considerable debate on choice of technologies

Second five-year plan (1967–71)
- use of development models to articulate socio-economic goals, potential growth patterns, major constraints, investment programmes
- focus on lead sectors (range of choice was extremely small, mainly because of capital requirements)
- necessary infrastructure

Third five-year plan (1972–76)
- economies of scale in agriculture and social services
- newer and higher-level technologies (survival or extinction in the face of ever-increasing international competition)

Building the technical infrastructure
- identify needs and capabilities before formulating the plan
- assess absorptive capacity for technology – institutional, legal, cultural, environmental and ecological factors
- strengthen key institutions – Ministry of Science and Technology, Institute of Science and Technology, Advanced Institute of Science, vocational training institutes, technical schools, associated legislation

Integrating urban development with rural development
- land reforms
- credit and technical advice for farmers
- community programmes, from digging sewage ditches to applying new agricultural techniques
- selective rural industrialization
- upgrading living conditions
- support to 20,000 villages, dependent on self-help
- transformation of local bureaucracies, driven by the head of state

Source: Derived from Choi (1979)

own advantage. China's development has already begun to echo that of the rest of East Asia, based on the similarly interventionist policies which it applied before joining the WTO, some of which it continues to apply. The country is regularly lambasted by Western trade officials for adopting policies which, they claim, break the rules. Growth in India and Brazil has been somewhat slower, but they too are big enough to stand up for themselves. No negotiated agreement is likely to slow the economic development of these three countries. Smaller and weaker ones whose industries have yet to become established are less well placed.

Developing countries that have been able to pursue trade-distorting policies as part of an export-oriented industrialization strategy have achieved increases in economic welfare two or three orders of magnitude bigger than the static efficiency effects of traditional trade theory. If every low-income country were able to do the same their economic gains would be considerable. The social effects would be complex, but poverty might begin to fall across the entire world as quickly as it has in East Asia and now China. It would not necessarily be sustainable. The associated environmental problems would also be similar to China's.

OVERALL IMPACT ON SUSTAINABLE DEVELOPMENT

We will not be able to draw any final conclusions about the overall impact on globally sustainable development of liberalizing trade in manufactured goods until we have seen how it interacts with all the other components of the negotiation agenda. At this stage the signs are not promising.

One good thing can be said for manufacturing liberalization. Industrialized countries have a tendency to make things worse for each other, and themselves, by waging trade wars with each other. That would be stopped, at least for manufactured goods. Other useful gains come from economies of scale, but only the industrial countries and newly industrializing ones benefit. No one benefits to any significant degree from the economic efficiency gains. These have traditionally been claimed as the main benefit of free trade, but the computerized methods that have been developed for estimating their magnitude have revealed that they are far smaller than expected.

These limited gains to a limited number of countries come at the cost of considerable disruption in all countries, rich and poor, as labour is shed from some sectors of the economy to be taken up, sooner or later or maybe not at all, in other sectors. Low-income countries whose government revenue comes largely from taxes on imports have to find some other way of finding the money they spend on health, education, environmental protection and social support. In many of the poorer countries, particularly in sub-Saharan Africa, manufacturing employment falls from levels that are already low. In some of the larger and more advanced developing countries, notably China, manufacturing wages go up. Elsewhere they go down. The countries that have found it hardest to lift people out of poverty through industrial development lose much of the chance to even try.

In parallel, climate change gets worse. Not a lot worse, but worse. Industrial production in some sectors moves from rich countries where it is well regulated to poor ones where regulation is much more difficult. In those countries pollution goes up, hazardous wastes go up and depletable water resources go down.

Some of these gains and losses to economies, people and the natural environment are made bigger or smaller by the interactions between what happens in urban areas and what happens in rural ones. It is the rural areas to which we now turn, with the impacts of the negotiations on agriculture.

5 | FOOD FOR THOUGHT

The country that cannot feed itself but depends on somebody else to put groceries on its table is enslaved. (Senator Mike Huckabee)[9]

The liberalization of agricultural trade is the opposite of that for manufactured goods, in that many developing countries promote it while US and European negotiators resist it.

In this chapter we examine the likely impacts. The elimination of export subsidies makes a positive contribution to sustainable development, but most of the other reforms do the opposite. Most people become more dependent on food imports, in both rich countries and poor ones. In poor ones the urban poor become even more vulnerable to fluctuations in world prices. Exports go up in some developing countries, but most of the benefit is reaped by big commercial farmers rather than smallholders. In most cases poverty goes up instead of down. Development strategies that have been particularly successful in reducing poverty in the past become much harder to pursue. Local environments improve in some countries and deteriorate in others. The global effects are almost all negative. The loss of biodiversity accelerates, carbon sinks shrink more rapidly, and climate change gets significantly worse.

TRADE IN AGRICULTURAL PRODUCTS

Towards the end of the sixteenth century Portuguese and Dutch traders began importing a delicacy known in China as *tcha*, and elsewhere in Asia as tay or tea. By the middle of the seventeenth century the new drink had become fashionable among the Dutch settlers of New Amsterdam (now New York), and was being served as an exotic alternative in the coffee houses of Rome, London and Vienna. By the middle of the eighteenth century it had transformed English culture to become the country's national drink, enjoyed in the polite cupful or sturdy mugful by rich and poor alike. It was just as popular in America. When the British government extended the East India Company's monopoly in the tea trade to America and introduced a tax, the colonists dumped the company's Chinese tea in Boston harbour to trigger their War of Independence. Britain then went to war with China to open its ports to free trade, enabling it to pay for its growing purchases of

Chinese tea by selling Chinese citizens the opium it produced in India. In parallel Britain had started a worldwide industrial revolution by processing cotton imported from America, whose exports of cotton, sugar and tobacco were grown by cheap labour shipped as slaves from Africa. The impacts of international trade in agricultural products can be very significant indeed.

Britain's abolition of agricultural protectionism with the 1846 repeal of its Corn Laws lasted less than a century. After the calamities of the First World War and the stock market crash of 1929 protective barriers were reintroduced in Britain, America and much of the rest of the world. The Second World War further heightened concerns for food security and led to the subsidies and import protection of Europe's Common Agricultural Policy and America's Farm Bill. Similar measures were introduced in other countries. The precursor to the WTO, the General Agreement on Tariffs and Trade (GATT), focused on manufactured goods and left these barriers to free trade in agricultural products largely untouched. They were addressed more fully in the Uruguay Round, with its 1994 Agreement on Agriculture. This included commitments to reduce subsidies, to convert non-tariff barriers to tariffs and to reduce tariffs, with sufficient ambiguity to limit their effectiveness. The WTO Doha agenda aimed to remove these ambiguities and achieve further liberalization beyond the 1994 agreement.

In negotiations to liberalize manufacturing trade the main proponents are the industrialized countries, opposed by developing ones. For agriculture the positions are reversed. The pressure for agricultural liberalization comes mainly from developing countries, supported by a few developed ones that are large agricultural exporters. Most of the opposition comes from the United States and Europe, supported by Japan.

This chapter examines the likely consequences of fully liberalizing agricultural trade on a worldwide basis. Implementation of the Uruguay Round's Agreement on Agriculture led to renegotiation of several other agreements, particularly between Europe and its former colonies in Africa, the Caribbean and the Pacific (the ACP countries). This has a strong influence on the impacts of multilateral liberalization through the WTO.

TRADITIONAL ECONOMIC GAINS FROM LIBERALIZING AGRICULTURAL TRADE

About two-thirds of the economic benefit that has been traditionally expected from free trade in goods comes from agriculture. On average the modelling studies indicate that removing all agricultural tariffs and subsidies would give a worldwide gain in economic welfare of about US$80 billion. For the more limited liberalization of the Doha negotiations this would come down to about $25 billion. Most exporting countries would gain, both developed and developing, with the largest share going to the developed ones. Developing countries as a whole would lose. The gains and losses are bigger than for manufacturing but still very small. The overall global gain of $80 billion corresponds to about 0.3 per cent of world net income. Over the ten years or more that it takes to negotiate and implement a trade agreement, the impact of full liberalization would be about a hundredth of what can be expected from normal economic growth. For the proposals tabled in Hong Kong this came down to less than one three hundredth.

Advocates of free trade tend to quote the numbers of billions of dollars involved without bothering to evaluate their significance. Trade negotiators do the same when trying to persuade other countries to accept their proposals, while ignoring the effect on economic welfare in their own countries. Other issues are far more important. The loss of tariff revenues can have significant adverse impacts in some of the poorest countries, but is only about a quarter of the effect for manufacturing. The main interest of trade negotiators in all countries is the much bigger impact on individual export industries and domestic producers, and in some cases the long-term dynamic effects.

PRICES AND PRODUCTION

Agricultural support reduces the price of exported food as well as the price at home. This provides a benefit to importing countries, paid for by the ones that give the support. When a country removes its subsidies the higher domestic food price is compensated by lower taxes, so that the net effect on the country's own consumers is small. The impact in the countries that import the food is much bigger, since the benefit of the subsidy is completely lost. In countries such as Egypt that are highly dependent on imports, the most immediate impact of agricultural liberalization is a rise in the price of food. This mainly affects urban areas, but can have indirect effects on rural ones as well.

The estimated change in world food prices is fairly small compared with more general fluctuations, but it has lasting effects on production. In any particular country production will tend to go up when other countries remove their subsidies and protective barriers, and down when it removes its own. The net effect depends on the country's initial level of protection and the extent to which it exports or imports agricultural produce. Six main groups are most affected: high-income countries with high levels of protection (such as those in the EU, the USA and Japan); others that are highly competitive exporters (Australia, New Zealand and Canada); major exporting developing countries (such as Brazil and Argentina); highly protected developing countries (such as China, India and Egypt); the least developed countries (mainly in sub-Saharan Africa); and other low-income developing countries (most of the rest of sub-Saharan Africa).

As with manufacturing, the small impact on economic welfare is the net effect of production changes that are much bigger. The modelling studies that we reviewed indicate that for full liberalization total agricultural and food output would go down by about 12 per cent in the EU and 18 per cent in Japan.[10] In the USA total production stays fairly constant, but cotton goes down by around 15 per cent, rice by 36 per cent and oilseeds 46 per cent. There are big production falls for some products in the EU too. Meat and dairy products go down by 18 per cent, oilseeds by 27 per cent, sugar by 43 per cent, grains by 48 per cent and cotton by 70 per cent. In Japan livestock production goes down by 26 per cent, rice, oilseeds, meat and dairy products by about 40 per cent, and sugar by 59 per cent. In Australia and New Zealand the opposite happens. Total agricultural and food output goes up by about 20 per cent, and by somewhat less in Canada.

Much of the extra food imported into Europe, the USA and Japan comes from Brazil and Argentina, particularly Brazil, where total output goes up by about 34 per cent. In the rest of Latin America it goes up by about 12 per cent. The volume of exports from other developing countries is smaller, but with big production changes for some products. Oilseed production is estimated to rise by 70 per cent in South Africa and 24 per cent in the rest of sub-Saharan Africa. In Mexico it goes down by 70 per cent. Sugar goes up by around 50 per cent in Central America, 47 per cent in East Africa, 32 per cent in South Africa and 29 per cent in the rest of sub-Saharan Africa. It falls sharply in Mauritius and Jamaica, which lose their preferential treatment for exports to the EU. Production of meat and dairy products goes up by about 15 per cent in the Middle East and North Africa, 12 per cent in South Africa and 45 per cent in the rest of sub-Saharan Africa. Grain production goes up by about 15 per cent in South Africa and down by 17 per cent in Mexico.

None of these global shifts in production suggests that liberalization would provide any more food for anyone anywhere, least of all in developing countries. Their resources would be diverted into producing more of it for Europe, America and Japan. Across the world the removal of high-income countries' agricultural support steers activity into other sectors and reduces the economic incentive to grow food. According to World Bank calculations full liberalization would reduce the world's total agricultural and food output by 1.3 per cent (Anderson et al. 2006).

These conventional economic equilibrium calculations are only part of the story. They reveal only that the production changes associated with agricultural liberalization are far more significant than the efficiency gains they are supposed to deliver.

FOOD SECURITY

Liberalization aims to increase international trade in agricultural products, and hence, by definition, to increase food imports and reduce the proportion produced at home. In some countries the domestic proportion goes up, but for the world as a whole it goes down. Even in countries where overall agricultural production rises, it falls for some products, with a corresponding rise in imports. High-income countries as a whole become less self-sufficient. It is estimated that with full liberalization their surplus in wheat would fall from 137 per cent of consumption to 118 per cent (ibid.). The surplus in oilseeds turns into a large deficit, with production falling from 119 per cent of consumption to 55 per cent. For rice the self-sufficiency ratio falls from 97 per cent to 49 per cent, and for sugar from 92 per cent to 47 per cent. For some individual countries the changes will be smaller and in others they will be bigger.

As measured by total food production and consumption, developing countries as a whole appear to become more self-sufficient. Much of the increase in production is for export, however. This includes products such as cut flowers and other products aimed specifically at export markets, and so self-sufficiency in domestic consumption may fall. The decline can be large for particular products. China's self-sufficiency in sugar falls from an already low 45 per cent to an even lower 27 per cent. In sub-Saharan Africa the ratio for vegetable oils and fats goes down from 85 per cent to 72 per cent, for rice from 91 per cent to 78 per cent, and for wheat from 53 per cent to 35 per cent.

As Nobel Prize-winning economist Amartya Sen has made clear, food self-sufficiency is not the same as food security. If imports can somehow be guaranteed, food security can be achieved without a country having to grow its own food. Sen argues that even the poorest of democracies such as India do not experience famines, because their governments will ensure that sufficient food is available from somewhere (Sen 1982). This is not always so in practice, even in democratic India. The country has not experienced a famine on the scale of the Great Bengal Famine of 1942, but smaller ones have occurred in Orissa, Andhra Pradesh, Uttar Pradesh, Madhya Pradesh, Maharashtra, Bihar and Gujarat (Shiva 2002). The policies to address rural poverty that were introduced with independence were subsequently reversed through structural adjustment programmes that the democratic system could do nothing to prevent. Sen argues that if Europe and America were to open their borders to India's agricultural exports, the poor would become rich enough to buy more food (Sen 1982). It is hard to see how the rural poor can become less poor by selling their agricultural produce to Europe and America and buying it back again.

Europe's Common Agricultural Policy and America's Farm Bill were introduced primarily for food security purposes. Following their experience in two world wars, particularly Europe's, their agricultural support serves mainly to ensure that no opponent can starve them to defeat in any other. Saudi Arabia has found an alternative way of avoiding reliance on world markets. It is now securing its food supplies by buying land or long-term leases in countries such as Egypt, Ethiopia and Sudan. China is doing the same in Congo and Zambia (Economist 2009b). The governments of the selling countries claim that fertile land is abundant and that their laws and policies protect the interests of local communities. In many cases both claims have been shown to be false (Cotula et al. 2009).

Food-importing countries that are not rich enough to buy land elsewhere import their food at prices that go up or down with the vagaries of the global market. In the world food price shock of 2008 the average food price went up by 78 per cent. The price of soyabeans and rice went up by over 130 per cent (Economist 2009b). Fluctuations in world prices have only minor effects on households whose expenditure on basic foods is a small proportion of their incomes. The impact on poor ones is big. The 2008 crisis triggered street demonstrations in India and Latin America, riots in Africa and emergency protective measures that contributed to yet another collapse of the Doha negotiations. Self-sufficiency in food may be a minor issue in an ideal world of economic stability, no international conflict and perfect markets. In a non-ideal one it is the top priority.[11]

ENERGY SECURITY AND BIOFUELS

As well as resisting the removal of their protective measures for agriculture in general, the USA and Europe have kept them high for biofuels. The use of crops to produce fuel instead of food was one of several contributory factors in the 2008 food price shock. Agricultural liberalization would make little difference in that respect. Biofuel production in the USA and Europe would go down, to be replaced by imports from other countries. Total production and its impact on world food prices would stay relatively unchanged.

Subsidies and other government incentives for producing biofuels serve two main purposes. They help to tackle climate change, and they help to reduce dependence on imported fossil fuels. Europe's policy statements put more emphasis on the first while America focuses on the second. Their actual policies are broadly similar. Both subsidize their own biofuel production and apply tariff barriers to imports.

Various crops can be used to produce biofuels, of which ethanol produced from sugar cane is the most competitive. Neither Europe nor America has a climate suited to sugar cane. The USA produces ethanol from maize, while Europe produces biodiesel from rapeseed and ethanol from sugar beet. Other feedstocks include soybean, palm oil and other oil crops. The development of 'second generation' technologies would improve the efficiency of many feedstocks, including sugar cane, but the new technologies are not expected to make a significant contribution before 2015 at the earliest, and Brazilian ethanol would still have the economic advantage. At present European biodiesel is competitive with oil at around $US72 a barrel, whereas Brazilian ethanol competes at $US35 (Motaal 2008). Ethanol produced in the USA from wheat is cheaper than European biodiesel, but is still over 50 per cent more expensive than the Brazilian fuel (Doornbosch and Steenblik 2007). Brazil has considerable capacity for expansion. If the market were fully liberalized other countries would find it hard to sell any more than the shortfall left by Brazilian production failing to expand fast enough to meet expanding world demand.

The cost of ethanol from sugar cane is sufficiently below that of other biofuels to give a significant overall economic benefit from trade liberalization. Producers in the USA and Europe would lose, but consumers would gain more. As we will see below, the environmental impacts are a long way short of being entirely positive whatever the feedstock. The main motive for maintaining subsidies and protectionist policies for biofuels is neither economic nor environmental. It is energy security.

EMPLOYMENT, INCOMES AND WORKING CONDITIONS

Agriculture in high-income countries is highly mechanized, with relationships between production and employment that are broadly similar to those for manufacturing. Employment in any particular sector will go up or down roughly in proportion to production. Full liberalization would reduce the total number of agricultural workers in Europe and Japan by between 10 and 20 per cent, concentrated in regions where the affected products are grown. In the USA, where overall production stays fairly constant, employment goes down in some regions and up in others, and workers have to relocate. In most high-income countries many of the workers affected are short-term migrants, so there will be knock-on effects on employment in their own countries, and a decline in the remittances they send back home. In Australia, New Zealand and other countries where overall production rises, the demand for agricultural labour rises.

Some of the most significant adverse impacts on incomes in industrialized countries are experienced by the recipients of agricultural subsidies. The biggest share goes to companies and individuals who own large commercial farms, but small farmers in less productive regions are also affected. Agricultural employment is only a few per cent of the total, so the impact on overall employment levels is small. The main impacts are relatively localized, and comparable to those which occur as other sectors of the economy expand or contract.

The impacts in developing countries are more complex. The number of people working in agriculture is a much larger proportion of the total (over 50 per cent in many countries) and so the impacts on people are much bigger. Computer models are often used to support arguments that trade liberalization would lift millions of people out of poverty. Their mathematical equations are a vast oversimplification. Most of the models examine only the formal economy, and not the informal one in which many of the poor survive. Even for the formal economy the models generally assume full employment, such that anyone who loses a job in one sector will automatically be employed in another. They treat unskilled labour as an amorphous mass, as though there were no difference between a subsistence farmer in one part of the country and a factory worker thousands of miles away. In practice the effects of the trade reforms are far more complex than the models are capable of calculating (Polaski 2006).

In countries and regions where production is projected to fall, total agricultural employment will fall. In those such as China and Vietnam where manufacturing is expanding it is likely to absorb the available labour reasonably quickly. In those where manufacturing is uncompetitive, particularly in Africa, both rural and urban unemployment will rise. Even in countries such as Brazil and Argentina where agricultural production expands it will not necessarily benefit the majority of rural people. Where rural unemployment is low, wage rates can be expected to rise. This may not be the case where unemployment is high, or when other factors influence the labour market (IAASTD 2009a). In most developing countries many of the rural poor rely on traditional food production for household use or sold locally for local consumption. Landholdings are small, with low productivity and limited access to distant markets. This traditional activity often coexists with more highly mechanized commercial agriculture, using higher-intensity inputs and less labour, often owned by city-based companies, producing internationally marketable produce.

In countries where exports rise the additional output will be produced mainly on farms that are best equipped to comply with other countries' food standards and get their products to market. This favours large-scale commercial farms rather than small-scale farmers. Wages and working conditions may be no improvement on what the newly employed workers were doing before. In Brazil the use of forced labour in cattle ranching has remained a persistent problem despite the efforts of government to stamp it out (Costa 2009). In Uzbekistan there have been widespread reports of the use of child labour for the production of cotton (EJF 2005). In such circumstances the expansion of commercial agriculture may serve only to expand its inequities.

Further adverse impacts can occur from the higher incentives for commercial farms to increase their land use. In countries like Brazil this can displace indigenous peoples and reduce the land available for traditional farming. Even in countries where production rises the overall result may be a fall in rural livelihood opportunities, with higher poverty levels and increased migration to the cities in search of alternatives. In those where manufacturing is thriving many of the migrants will earn higher wages than are available in rural areas. Elsewhere they may have to eke out a living in the city slums.

The changes in production patterns can have differential impacts on women. In many developing countries a large proportion of rural women work in traditional food production and are unpaid. The commercial farms that are most likely to benefit from increased export opportunities tend to employ a smaller proportion of women, and hire them as waged labour. Depending on local cultural factors, some export products such as fruit and flowers may employ a larger female workforce, but in conditions that may be less healthy and provide a poorer standard of living than traditional agriculture.

All these different impacts on different people in different countries occur in the short to medium term as a direct consequence of the production changes. The longer-term dynamic effects are different again. In the short to medium term at least, however, the removal of agricultural subsidies and import barriers by high-income countries would not provide the universal benefit to people in developing countries that is often assumed. It is more likely to do the opposite.

ENVIRONMENTAL IMPACTS

Agriculture can have as big an impact on the natural environment as any other human activity. It deliberately replaces biological diversity with a few selected species. It consumes water, which may be in short supply. It uses insecticides, pesticides and herbicides, which generate pollution and are specifically intended to kill other species. Fertilizers can pollute too, and can have catastrophic effects on local ecosystems. Overproduction may cause erosion and reduce the fertility of the soil, reducing its value for agriculture or anything else. Over-abstraction of water has the same effect, by increasing the salinity of aquifers and then the soil. Cattle produce methane, a much stronger greenhouse gas than carbon dioxide. Forest conversion releases greenhouse gases, and either destroys or reduces the effectiveness of some of the biggest carbon sinks. All of these impacts can in principle be managed, and kept within acceptable bounds. At the global level they never have been, either for biodiversity loss or for greenhouse gas emissions. At the local level the effectiveness of management is highly variable, in rich countries as well as poor ones.

Trade liberalization increases agricultural production in some areas, reducing it in others. Where production goes down the impacts go down, and where it goes up they get bigger. Except for diffuse effects such as greenhouse gas emissions, the gains and losses do not cancel each other out. Reduced pressure on one endangered species does not compensate for the loss of another. Less pollution of one person's drinking water does not make up for polluting someone else's. The beneficial impact of lower agricultural production in a region of low biological diversity is considerably smaller than the negative impact of a corresponding increase in a high-diversity one.

Increased production of food and biofuels in Brazil and other biodiversity-rich countries, for consumption in America, Europe, Japan and other high-income countries that have already destroyed most of their own biological diversity, would not necessarily have adverse environmental impacts of any great significance. Brazil has made great strides in improving agricultural efficiency through technological developments that increase the yields from a given area and keep pollution levels low.

It is possible that ongoing developments might enable the country to accommodate the estimated 34 per cent increase in its agricultural production with no adverse effects. It would be remarkable if they did (see Box 5.1). The situation is similar to that for the impacts of manufacturing in China. Despite the efficiency improvements, the Amazon rainforest and other diversity-rich areas have continued to shrink. Unless these trends can be reversed, agricultural liberalization would add considerably to environmental problems that are already severe.

In countries such as Brazil where land is abundant, the extensification of agriculture on to new land is usually cheaper than increasing production through more intensive use of inputs. The Amazon region itself is unsuitable for the production of sugar cane, and deforested land is used mainly for cattle and, to a lesser extent, soya. On top of the predicted increase in exports, soya production will rise further to provide more cattle feed. If more land were to be taken for the expansion in beef it would affect the Amazon directly. The expansion of sugar cane and soya would affect it indirectly by taking land used for beef. Similar effects occur in Argentina and other countries where agricultural output rises and biodiversity is high.

Significant biodiversity impacts also occur from the expected increase in production in Australia and New Zealand, along with greater salinization and soil acidification. In countries and regions where access to new land is constrained, increases in production are likely to require greater use of agrochemicals. This is particularly the case where liberalization causes commercial farms to expand and traditional farming to contract. Additional environmental hazards come from greater economic incentives for the use of transgenic crops. Though some transgenic varieties reduce the use of agrochemicals, others increase it. This comes in parallel with highly uncertain and potentially disastrous impacts associated with transfer of genes to wild relatives and the resilience of whole ecosystems (IAASTD 2009b; CIPR 2002).

Except where sugar or cotton expand or contract most of the environmental impacts in the least developed countries and other African low-income countries are fairly marginal. Existing environmental pressures are relieved where production goes down, and are heightened where it goes up.

In the EU and Japan the environmental impacts are generally beneficial. There will be a negative influence on the amenity value of agriculture as production declines, but in high-income countries this is readily countered through appropriate rural and regional policies. Pressure on biological diversity will fall. In global terms the effect falls far short of

---

BOX 5.1 AGRICULTURE AND FORESTRY IN BRAZIL

Brazil's natural forest areas, principally those of the Amazon basin, are of exceptional ecological importance in global terms. Cattle ranching and soybean production have direct and indirect links to the deforestation of large areas. Both industries have seen exceptional growth, and Brazil now ranks as the world's second-largest exporter of soybean and bovine meat. Significant potential exists for expansion.

Economic modelling of the proposed EU–Mercosur trade agreement indicates that it would lead to a 32 per cent growth in agricultural production. Multilateral liberalization through the WTO would lead to further growth. At current rates of efficiency an increase of 32 per cent would need an extra 55 million hectares of land to be brought into productive use, with beef responsible for the vast majority. Some of the increased output would be met through increased efficiency, for which there is considerable scope. Increased efficiency would increase profitability, however, which may lead to further deforestation. Intensification may therefore have only a limited effect on land take, such that growth in output will be predominantly met through the utilization of new land.

The greatest relative increase in soybean and cattle production has occurred in states that are either within or adjacent to the Amazon region. A continuation of previous trends would further intensify production along the natural forest frontier, increasing pressure for forest conversion. Most of the land needed for increased soybean production may be accommodated on degraded

---

compensating for the opposite effect in the countries from which they import more food, whose biodiversity is much richer.

Climate change is reduced by some effects and increased by others. The increase in international transport causes an increase in global emissions of about 0.5 per cent for manufacturing and agriculture combined (see Chapter 5). The movements in production will cause carbon emissions to go up by about 3 per cent in Brazil and down by a similar amount in other countries. This does not include the potential contributions of biofuel liberalization to reducing climate change, or of deforestation to increasing it. As a replacement for fossil fuels Brazilian ethanol is far more effective in reducing greenhouse gas emissions

pasture rather than forested land, which can help to restore pasture soils through nitrogen fixation. This pattern of production, however, alongside the considerable expansion in cattle livestock, may have an indirect effect on natural forest conversion through indirect mechanisms. A continuation of the trend for consolidation of smaller farm units into larger agro-industrial enterprises using less labour is likely to displace smaller farmers. This leads to increased urbanization, and also to resettlement on previously uncultivated land.

Much of the new settlement may occur through illegal invasions of forested areas. These are attractive to settlers because degraded pasture can be difficult to farm by hand. Additionally, clearing forest for agriculture brings an initial economic gain from the timber, and improves the settler's claim to the settled land. Current Brazilian legislation allows settlers to deforest 20 per cent of their land and maintain 80 per cent as legal reserve, and 50 per cent of forest defined as 'under transition' can also be cleared. It has been estimated, however, that the law is violated on between 60 to 70 per cent of settled land. Illegal felling is difficult to monitor, so in practice a much higher proportion of natural forest may be felled. Further pressure on forest areas may also occur through transportation infrastructure projects, which are essential for opening up previously inaccessible areas, and which have typically led to further frontier colonization and exploitation by other actors.

Source: Adapted from Nelson and Ryder (2007)

than biofuels grown in Europe or the USA. According to some recent estimates, most or all of the production in Europe and America might even increase emissions.[12] The environmental benefit of liberalization would be lost completely, however, if sugar cane production were to push beef or soya into the Amazon. A rise in world prices in 1999 led to rising production in Brazil that contributed to a 33 per cent increase in the rate of deforestation over the next five years. A repeat would have major adverse effects on climate change as well as global biodiversity. Deforestation currently causes about 18 per cent of total global greenhouse gas emissions (Stern 2006).

Many of the environmental impacts of agricultural liberalization are relatively localized, with beneficial effects in some areas and adverse ones in others. The global impacts are almost certain to be large and adverse. The effect on climate change could be positive, but unless biofuel production is managed extraordinarily well it is more likely to be negative and large. Food production for European, American and Japanese consumers moves out of their own countries, where biodiversity has already been reduced dramatically, into others whose still-surviving natural habitats are major stabilizers of the global climate and whose biodiversity is still of major global importance. Liberalization of agricultural trade threatens to destroy that too.

DYNAMIC EFFECTS

The World Bank's *World Development Report* for 2008 placed a welcome renewed emphasis on the role of agriculture in development (World Bank 2007). It pointed out that in developing countries three out of every four poor people live in rural areas, and that the Millennium Development Goal of halving world poverty by 2015 cannot possibly be met without a focus on rural needs. The report's prescriptions have been less well received. Some commentators have criticized them for adjusting the evidence of past success to fit the Bank's policies rather than the other way round. Others have been equally damning of the report's promotion of agribusiness and its focus on free market competition, market-based land reforms, the privatization of agricultural research and the liberalization of trade, while paying lip-service to the role of traditional farmers (ActionAid 2007; Oxfam 2007; Ecofair 2007).

The industrial revolution that transformed Britain from a low-income economy to a high-income one would not have been possible without a parallel revolution in agriculture. This enabled more food to be produced by fewer people and released others to work in manufacturing. Much the same happened subsequently in the rest of Europe and North America, then Japan, and then in the newly emerging economies of East Asia. China is now following suit, in a dynamic process of transformation that can be stopped dead in its tracks by trade liberalization. The transformation has not always been painless. In Britain, where market forces had free rein, many of the farm workers who became surplus to requirements were reduced to the industrial city squalor that turned Marx and Engels into revolutionaries. Most of the rest emigrated to America. Today's developing countries do not have the second option and would sooner avoid the first.

East Asia has managed its transition from low-productivity to high-productivity agriculture considerably better than Britain did. So has

China. As the World Bank readily acknowledges, progress towards the Millennium Development Goal for world poverty would be minimal were it not for China's remarkable success. Research by the Bank's own staff (Ravallion 2008) indicates that this was achieved through policies that differed markedly from those promoted in its flagship report. Market competition did indeed play a key role, but only between small farmers. Large farms, in the form of collectives, were scrapped. Responsibility for agriculture was shifted from large organizations to small ones, empowering the rural poor. Individual households were granted land rights rather than ownership, ensuring that a relatively equal allocation of landholdings was maintained. Agricultural research institutions were established that were responsible not to companies but to the state, with sufficient influence to persuade policy-makers at the highest level to act on the research findings. Subsequent central policies were often scaled-up versions of successful local initiatives taken by farmers themselves. Those policies might well have failed had it not been for China's tradition of building and maintaining the administrative capacities of government at every level down to the village. Rural industry was promoted in parallel. High levels of rural literacy had already been established, equipping people for employment in manufacturing as the labour productivity of agriculture rose. It was not until all of this was in place that China embarked on the trade reforms that were needed for WTO membership.

China's record over the past few decades has been rightly criticized on human rights issues. Its dramatic contribution to reducing world poverty is uncontested. Its home-grown strategy followed the example set by the tiger economies of East Asia. They too achieved dramatic improvements in both agricultural productivity and poverty reduction, not by focusing on agriculture or on manufacturing, but through integrated rural–urban development strategies that combined the two (Ali 2004). Korea's transformation was among the most impressive (see Box 4.1). Its rural development programme through the 1970s and 1980s involved many different types of intervention, which changed as the overall national economy changed (Choi 1986). In parallel with land reforms, economically viable industries were established in rural areas, with close links between agriculture and industry. High priority at the national level was given to developing rural infrastructure. At first government incentives were given to farmers to improve their own living environments. Villagers were then assisted with building farm roads, small-scale irrigation schemes, building village meeting halls and setting up credit unions. Support then moved to income-generating projects such as group farming, common seedbeds, off-season vegetable cultivation, new pasturage, community forestation, local processing factories and common marketing systems. Encouragement of cottage industries was complemented by the promotion of rural–urban linkage industries, producing component parts or semi-processed goods for large firms in urban areas. These were given special advantages such as guaranteed markets and a supply of necessary technologies from parent companies. Other industries were decentralized into rural areas to create employment, maximize the use of rural resources and alleviate urban pollution. Trade barriers were maintained until the mid-1980s, when both agriculture and manufacturing had become globally competitive.

Strategies such as these are not easy to implement. If a country exposes itself to global competition before it has become competitive the task becomes almost impossible. Subsidies in high-income countries have the same effect, particularly when accompanied by trade rules that prohibit import barriers being raised to counter them. Export subsidies are particularly pernicious. Cheap subsidized food imported from the USA and Europe benefits urban consumers, at the expense of local farmers. This is no great problem in highly productive countries like Brazil, where the respective roles of large- and small-scale agriculture are conditioned mainly by domestic policy. It is primarily in Africa and parts of South Asia that current international policies stop traditional farmers emulating the East Asian success.

OVERALL IMPACT ON SUSTAINABLE DEVELOPMENT

As with manufacturing trade the impacts of liberalizing agriculture are mixed. Except for the elimination of export subsidies the effects are far less beneficial to people in developing countries than is often assumed, and in the short term even here it has adverse effects. The welfare gains from economic efficiency are bigger than for manufactures, but are still very small compared with normal rates of economic growth. Exports from developing countries to developed ones go up, but the benefit goes to big commercial farmers rather than small ones. The fundamental development problem of finding well-paid employment for the people whose livelihood opportunities are lost through increasing agricultural productivity gets worse rather than better. In the absence of a blossoming manufacturing sector to compensate, poverty goes up instead of down. The combined rural and urban development strategies that have proved so successful in reducing poverty in some parts of the world become impossible, with the small-scale farming systems at their heart displaced by large commercial operations. Their output goes up, not for consumption at home, but for export to consumers in richer parts of the world. The developed countries produce less of their own food and import more. Import dependency goes up everywhere. The urban poor become even more vulnerable to fluctuations in world food prices than they were already.

In some parts of the world local environments improve. In others they deteriorate, giving an overall effect in which biodiversity goes down. Unless some way is found of managing biodiversity-rich areas far better than they have ever been managed before, global biodiversity declines even faster than before, carbon sinks shrink even faster than before, and trade in biofuels amplifies the problem it is supposed to solve. Climate change then gets worse. Unlike with manufacturing liberalization, it gets a lot worse. Except for the elimination of export subsidies, the overall impact of agricultural liberalization on sustainable development is decidedly negative.

6 | INVISIBLE EARNINGS

> Probably more than three-fourths of the whole benefit she [England] has derived from the progress of manufactures during the nineteenth century has been through its indirect influences in lowering the cost of transport of men and goods, of water and light, of electricity and news. (Alfred Marshall)[13]

Service industries, particularly financial services, have come to play a major role in the economies of Europe and other high-income countries. Obtaining greater access to other countries' services markets is one of Europe's main offensive interests in trade negotiations, supported by the USA and other countries with strong service industries. Some developing countries have export interests for some types of service, but on the whole liberalization is promoted by developed countries and resisted by developing ones.

In this chapter we examine the likely impacts for each type of service. The effects vary considerably between them. The liberalization of telecommunications and transport services offers significant benefits, but with nothing to be gained from using them as bargaining chips in trade negotiations. Of the other service types only three pose serious problems. For distribution services the more affluent sections of society in developing countries tend to gain, while poorer ones lose and the environment loses. The potential environmental benefits from liberalizing environmental services are relatively small, and more than outweighed by the social and environmental costs. Efficient financial services benefit any country's economy, but most would do better to strengthen their own provision rather than rely on foreign suppliers and run the major risks of financial instability that have accompanied liberalization.

TRADE IN SERVICES

By the end of the nineteenth century the economist Alfred Marshall had already observed that England was well on the way to becoming a service economy. America and Germany had made major inroads into its near-monopoly in manufacturing. Three-quarters of England's industrial wealth now came from cheaper and more effective transport services, environmental services, energy supply services and communication services. A century later the whole of Europe had lost its pre-eminence in mass manufacturing. Countries that had once imported European goods were now producing their own and exporting them, to Europe, to America, and to all their former markets. Recognizing the threat to Europe's elevated position in 'the global economic league table', the European Union launched its Lisbon strategy, aiming to make it 'the most dynamic knowledge-based economy in the world' (European Commission 2004a: 12, 2005a: 3). Henceforth Europe's place in the globalized economy would be in the development and promotion of new technologies and high-value service industries.

The idea of a service economy is not new. England is the only country where manufacturing has ever employed a majority of the workforce, and then only briefly (Kumar 1978). Elsewhere services have always employed more people, and a major proportion when material goods have been imported. The ancient trading cities of Byblos in the Levant, Carthage, Athens and then Rome were primarily exporters of transport services and governmental services in return for imports of food and manufactures. Venice of the fifteenth and sixteenth centuries was a technologically based service economy par excellence, earning much of its considerable wealth from supplying shipping services and financial services to Europe, and, where it could reach it, the world. Much of industrializing Britain's wealth came not from manufacturing itself, but from buying, selling, financing and shipping the raw materials, the finished products and, in the case of the slave economies of America and the West Indies, the labour.

England's accumulating business capital was used to finance the ports, railways, warehouses, plantations and mines in the countries that supplied the materials and bought the finished goods. The process began long before the Industrial Revolution. John Maynard Keynes traced it back to 'the treasure which Drake stole from Spain in 1580' (Keynes 1963 [1930]). England's Queen Elizabeth I had funded the pirate ships with which Drake purloined the gold and silver that the conquistadors had stolen from the Aztecs and the Incas. She invested the proceeds in trading operations in the Middle East, whose profits were used to found the East India Company, which in turn provided the income for further infrastructural investment in Latin America, China, sub-Saharan Africa and the rest of the 'developing' world. In consequence Britain's ownership of foreign assets expanded a hundred-thousand-fold between 1580 and 1930. Britain developed. The countries it invested in did not.

Most high-income countries now operate a trade deficit in goods, importing more than they export. To maintain a neutral balance of payments they have to make up the deficit with earnings on services and other invisible exports. As imports of manufactured goods have risen, the liberalization of trade in financial and other services has played an increasing role in trade negotiations. Traditional trade economics theory says that everyone in every country should benefit. As with free trade in goods, the reality is a lot more complicated than the theory.

SERVICES NEGOTIATIONS

The WTO defines four modes by which services are supplied. Cross-border trade (mode 1) consists of transactions across the border itself, such as transport services. Consumption abroad (mode 2) occurs when the consumer is in the foreign country, such as for tourism or education. Commercial presence (mode 3) covers direct foreign investment, such as for delivering telecommunications or electricity supply services. Presence of natural persons (mode 4) covers temporary residence of a service exporter's employees, such as to manage the local office of a bank or provide consultancy. The WTO agreements specifically exclude fuller liberalization of the international labour market through migration or other long-term residence.

Barriers to services trade include limitations on the number of service suppliers, the volume of output, the value of transactions or assets, the number of people employed, the issue of visas or work permits, the participation of foreign capital and the types of organization that can supply a service. Any of these restrictions may contravene the basic principles of the WTO. These require that foreign suppliers should be treated no less favourably than domestic ones (national treatment), and that a product or service supplied by one member country is treated no less favourably than a similar one supplied by another (the most favoured nation rule). The General Agreement on Trade in Services (GATS) does not prohibit such constraints, but requires every member country to make specific commitments to providing equal treatment, and to define any limitations that may apply. These must be listed in a national schedule for all four modes of supply, covering both horizontal commitments for all services and others that apply only to particular service types. Some of the USA's regional and bilateral trade agreements differ from GATS in defining a list of exceptions to equal treatment rather than a list of commitments. Most of Europe's regional and bilateral agreements follow the GATS approach, and aim for more commitments than have been made through the WTO.

Negotiations over these agreements take place through a series of offers and requests in which countries define extra commitments that they are prepared to make themselves, and specify what they want in return. These form part of the negotiation of a single undertaking for the entire trade agenda. Any concessions given in other areas, such as for agriculture, typically depend on other countries making commitments in services which they would not otherwise make.

TRADITIONAL ECONOMIC GAINS

The effects of liberalizing services trade are harder to quantify than for physical goods. Statistics are poor, and the barriers are mainly qualitative and not easily expressed in numerical terms. This makes it extremely difficult to calculate the different effects of liberalizing different types of service. All estimates are highly speculative, and give only a rough indication of the possible size of the effects (Dihel 2002).

The modelling studies that we reviewed indicate that the worldwide gain in economic welfare could be as much as twice as high as for manufacturing and agriculture combined (Hertel and Keeney 2006; Decreux and Fontagné 2006; François et al. 2005). For full liberalization much of this would come from increased mobility of temporary labour under mode 4, particularly for semi-skilled and unskilled workers. This is one of the main requests of developing countries, and is strongly resisted by the developed ones. The total estimated gain for full liberalization amounts to about US$250 billion. This represents about 1 per cent of world net income, falling to around 0.3 per cent for the more limited ambitions of the Doha negotiations. Over a ten-year period a 1 per cent gain would be about a thirtieth of what can be expected from normal economic growth. A gain of 0.3 per cent is about a hundredth. This is higher than for manufacturing and agriculture, but still very small. Among developing countries, only India, South Africa and a few others with strong service industries are expected to gain more than the global average. Most would gain less.

Because the barriers to services trade are not in the form of tariffs, their removal does not cause any direct loss of government revenue. All the other economic, social and environmental impacts depend strongly on the type of service.

VARIETIES OF SERVICE INDUSTRY

Most service sector jobs bear no relation to Europe's dream of a knowledge-based economy. They consist of ordinary tasks such as cleaning streets or offices, cooking food or serving it, teaching children in school or fixing the plumbing. The trade liberalization agenda stops well short of promoting foreign competition for such work, content to leave the issues in the hands of the immigration authorities. The services of interest to exporters are only those that can be delivered through the WTO's modes 1, 2 and 3. Liberalization in mode 4, the movement of people, is limited to whatever temporary residence is needed for supplying services in the other three modes.

The WTO has categorized internationally tradable service industries in twelve main groups. These are business (including professional and computer) services; communication services; construction and related engineering services; distribution services; educational services; environmental services; financial (insurance and banking) services; health-related and social services; tourism and travel-related services; recreational, cultural and sporting services; transport services; other less significant services. Energy services are often treated as an extra category.

For some of these service industries the stakes are low. Liberalization of business and professional services usually involves a trade-off between the loss of domestic jobs and the lower costs or higher quality of foreign suppliers. Developing-country suppliers generally compete on cost, particularly for Internet-based services for which professional qualifications are not required. High-income countries compete on greater sophistication of the services offered.

Construction services and related engineering services involve similar trade-offs. The construction industry is well established in many developing countries, with highly experienced firms using modern techniques. Since salaries and wages are lower than in high-income countries they often have little to lose from opening their own markets, and much to gain from other countries opening theirs.

There have been cases where the liberalization of energy services has created serious problems, notably in major electricity supply scandals in India involving the now disgraced US company Enron (Zarrilli 2002). Such cases are fairly rare, and the benefits of liberalization are much clearer than they are for privatization. In Tunisia, which has maintained state control over build-operate-transfer contracts with foreign suppliers, energy costs have been reported as being a factor of two or more below those in African countries that have privatized their national electricity industries as well as liberalizing international trade in them (UNECA 2004).

Most educational services are provided by the public sector and are not affected by trade liberalization. No issues of great concern arise for private education. Concerns are somewhat higher for health and social services. A review by UNCTAD (1997) concluded that, except in the poorest countries, liberalization has had a beneficial effect by putting downward pressure on health service costs. Some developing countries gain economically from treating foreign patients or remittances from professionals working abroad (World Bank 2002). Unless a country has a strong healthcare system and a surplus of medical personnel, however, either activity can have significant adverse effects on the health of its own population (Hilary 2004).

Countries with strong media industries such as the United States and India promote liberalization of recreational, audiovisual, cultural and sporting services. The main concern here is the threat to cultural heritage. Tourism and travel-related services generate many concerns over environmental and social impacts, but these are not strongly influenced by trade liberalization. The growth of the industry is determined mainly by market opportunity and government policy, and the effects of liberalization are fairly small.

Most of the controversy over liberalizing services trade through GATS or regional agreements arises for the other five categories: financial, communication, environmental, transport and distribution.

FINANCIAL SERVICES

In the preparations for the Hong Kong ministerial meeting at the end of 2005 the EU, the USA and several other countries that export financial services presented a Joint Statement to the WTO proclaiming the benefits of liberalization. They supported their argument with the statement that, in its 2004 *World Investment Report*, 'UNCTAD concludes that in today's global economy, an internationally competitive services, including financial services, sector is essential for development' (WTO 2005). This was a somewhat cavalier description of what the report actually said. It did indeed conclude that 'an internationally competitive services sector is, in today's world economy, essential for development', but without the specific reference to financial services (UNCTAD 2004: 237). The UNCTAD report offered little to justify the Joint Statement's claim. It cited numerous studies suggesting that 'the entry of foreign financial institutions might undermine the ability of national authorities to exercise control over international capital movements into and out of their countries', that 'the risk of volatility in foreign-exchange flows may rise with the entry of international financial service providers', and that 'there is a possibility of contagion effects from foreign crises in the home market or third-country markets that are transmitted via the presence of foreign banks' (ibid.: 139).

The 2005 Joint Statement was more accurate in quoting the World Bank's 2001 report on *Finance for Growth* (World Bank 2001). It had indeed argued that an efficient financial sector, including foreign participation, is important for growth and stability. In drawing that conclusion the report cited Argentina as a prime example of the beneficial effects of foreign entry, both in improving the efficiency and competitiveness of local banking systems and in enhancing financial stability. A few months after the report was published the Argentinian economy collapsed.

The European Commission's contributors to the 2005 Joint Statement should have known better than to base their case for liberalization on that particular World Bank report. The impact assessment study on the WTO negotiations that was published on their own website in 2003 had already pointed out the folly of relying on it (George and Kirkpatrick 2003). It quoted the Bank's own former chief economist, Joseph Stiglitz, as arguing that, at least in part, the Argentinian crisis was caused by poorly managed liberalization of the country's banking system (Stiglitz 2002). Other research into the causes of the crisis has drawn similar conclusions (Damill and Frenkel 2003).

Irrespective of the dubious evidence presented by trade negotiators, the liberalization of financial services can have benefits. Detailed research by the World Bank has found that countries that have successfully reformed their financial services sectors, along with telecommunications, have on average grown about a percentage point faster than other countries (Mattoo 2005). There is no clear evidence whether openness has contributed to faster growth, or growth has stimulated greater openness, but other studies have found that the availability of efficient financial services is a key input to economic performance (Jalilian et al. 2007). The same World Bank research, however, warns that unless liberalization is accompanied by adequate prudential supervision, it can lead to poor investment decisions and have the opposite effect to that intended. Another study of the effects of past liberalization programmes reports large variations. Significant improvements in banking system performance were observed in three of the countries studied, but less positive experience in Korea and many African countries (Hodge 2002).

The poor experience of liberalization in Korea was closely associated with the East Asian economic collapse of 1997. Numerous other studies of the financial crises in Latin America and East Asia have concluded that liberalization in the absence of a proper policy framework can exacerbate instability in the financial sector or the whole economy (Finger and Schuknecht 1999; Key 1999; Contreras and Yi 2004; Daniel and Jones 2006; Bird and Rajan 2001). A study of twenty-six banking crises found that in eighteen cases the financial sector had recently been liberalized. Other potential hazards of poorly managed financial services liberalization have also been reported (Stiglitz 2002; UNDP/ Rockefeller 2003; Stiglitz and Charlton 2004; UNCTAD 2004): large foreign-owned banks may crowd out domestic banks from the most creditworthy customers, domestic banks may fail by taking on high-risk business in response, SMEs may find it harder to obtain credit, the banking system may be less likely to address gaps in the credit system for disadvantaged social groups or regions, the banking system may be less amenable to monetary policies designed to avoid booms and slumps, and profit repatriation may put pressure on a country's balance of payments (Stiglitz 2002; UNDP/Rockefeller 2003; Stiglitz and Charlton 2004; UNCTAD 2004). Some of these effects also have adverse gender impacts, since women in poor countries are more likely than men to be excluded from the formal sector, and are more strongly dependent on small-scale borrowing.

All of these concerns have increased dramatically since the world financial crisis of 2008. Among others Pascal Lamy, as director general of the WTO, has called for a global system of financial rules, asserting that the crisis has shown that purely national solutions are not enough (CENTAD 2008). The IMF is not so sure. Its Global Financial Stability Report for 2008 calls only for better coordination among financial overseers, while advising developing countries to focus their policy actions on lowering their vulnerabilities to knock-on effects from the developed ones (IMF 2008). Dani Rodrik gives three reasons for why Lamy is wrong and the IMF right (Rodrik 2009). First, he finds it hard to imagine that the US Congress would ever agree to the kind of intrusive international oversight that might have prevented the sub-prime crisis, let alone avert any future ones. Weaker developing countries might be cajoled into surrendering sovereignty, but not America, and probably not Europe either, nor China. Second, even if the leading nations were to agree, they might easily adopt a uniformly wrong set of regulations. None of them understands the crisis well enough to be sure of what to do about it. Most importantly, appropriate forms of financial regulation differ between countries according to their circumstances and levels of development. To those three problems we can add the observation that the current crisis has extended up to the global level the contribution made by financial services liberalization to all the more localized financial crises catalogued above.

Before the global crisis the evidence for treating financial services liberalization with great caution was already strong. Now it is inescapable. Liberalization benefits the seller of the service, with enormous risks for the buyer.

COMMUNICATIONS SERVICES

International trade in communications services focuses mainly on telecommunications, which can play a major role in helping to transform a country's entire economy. The World Bank research noted above suggests that growth rates in countries that have liberalized both financial and telecommunications services have been about 1 per cent higher than elsewhere. The relatively weak statistical correlation noted in that study, however, reflects large variations. When India liberalized its telecommunications market in the mid-1990s, ineffective regulation created conflicts that delayed network expansion and adversely affected private investment (Hodge 2002). These difficulties in India have since been overcome. China's experience offers a different lesson. Its impressive economic growth has been associated with rapid expansion of the telecommunications sector, but without privatization or liberalization. Ambitious public investment in its state monopoly led to a more than tenfold expansion of the telecommunications network. In other countries monopolies have been less benign, whether state owned or privately owned (World Bank 2003b). In Morocco competition from a second supplier forced the incumbent to lower tariffs four times in one year. In Jordan the price of mobile telecommunications fell rapidly after the market was opened to competition from Egypt.

For most developing countries the telecommunications sector is one of the most likely to deliver significant benefits from liberalization. Few have the technical capability to follow China's example of modernizing the sector without foreign involvement, particularly in Africa, where the benefits of an expanding mobile phone network have been considerable (Scott et al. 2004). Strong regulation is necessary to avoid the difficulties experienced in India, but the systems need not be as sophisticated as for some service industries. In most cases the main benefits come not from within the telecommunications sector itself, but from its potential contribution to the performance of the whole economy.

ENVIRONMENTAL SERVICES

About 80 per cent of the environmental services market is for the provision of water supply, sanitation and solid waste disposal (Kirkpatrick et al. 2006b). The impacts of liberalizing trade in other environmental services such as air quality protection, remediation of contaminated land, noise abatement and the protection of biodiversity and landscape are fairly small. Most of the controversy is over water supply and sanitation.

The global market for water and waste-water services is dominated by a small number of multinational corporations. Five of these accounted for 45 per cent of private sector projects during the 1990s (World Bank 2003c). Trade liberalization has little or no effect on the entry of foreign firms when the service is provided by the public sector. Conversely, privatization often has little effect when trade barriers are maintained. The two go hand in hand in enabling market access for international companies. Privatization is promoted through conditionalities on debt relief and on loans from the IMF and the World Bank, and through aid given by donor governments for privatization programmes. Liberalization is promoted by the EU, the USA and other supplier countries through the WTO and other trade agreements.

One of the key targets of the Millennium Development Goals is to halve, by 2015, the proportion of people without sustainable access to safe drinking water and basic sanitation. This cannot be achieved without major investment in infrastructure, which is not easily provided by governments, particularly in poor countries. Development aid has contributed in the past, but far less than is needed. Loans from the World Bank have also contributed, but have to be paid back. In seeking a solution the Bank and other development agencies have turned to private sector finance, in the belief that this will improve efficiency enough to pay for itself. Research by the Bank's own staff casts doubt on that belief.

A World Bank review of water and sanitation reforms in Latin America concluded that the private sector had performed no worse than the public sector, and no better (Clarke et al. 2004). Research in Asia gave a similar result, finding no significant difference between public and private provision (Estache and Rossi 2002). Other research shows that while connection rates have often increased with privatization, this has often been restricted to more affluent users. Prices have often been raised above agreed levels within a few years, those who cannot pay have been disconnected, and they have been left to buy their essential needs from street vendors offering dubious quality at even higher prices (Mehta and la Cour Madsen 2005). In several cases the public outcry has been so great that governments have had to renationalize the service (UNDP 2009). When one of the European suppliers claimed compensation for the termination of its contract the claim was rejected by the World Bank, which had itself supported the privatization programme (Molina and Chowla 2008). When the company took the country's government to court it was found to be in breach of contract and lost the case. Meanwhile, many case studies have shown how reforms within the public sector have often been highly effective in improving supply to

BOX 6.1 PUBLIC SECTOR INITIATIVES IN WATER SUPPLY AND SANITATION

The conurbation of Rabat-Casablanca in Morocco has experienced a substantial drop in the rate of growth in water use for twelve years, in spite of high and growing urbanization, by using measures to repair and find leaks in the system, setting up a banded pricing system to make consumers – including public users – more responsible, and with welfare provision for the poor, but with the supply of water routinely metered, and an intense public awareness campaign for water saving. These actions have been made possible by an appropriate administrative framework that combines private business with government agencies and local authorities to give 'delegated management of the water services' but supported by a binding inter-authority charter. This has allowed costly investments (dams, water movement channels) to be deferred as these are difficult to finance without extra debts and in the end often prove not to be necessary.

Source: Plan Bleu 2003 (from DGH Rabat)

In Botswana, the Water Utilities Corporation (WUC) has been able to meet daily water requirements in all of its operational areas, including both urban and peri-urban areas. WUC substantially increased the proportion of the population with access to safe water over the period from 1970 to 1998. The population served increased from 30,000 to 330,000 while the average daily consumption rose.

In Bogotá, Colombia, privatization was rejected and effort put into improving the public water and sanitation provider. It became

poor communities while reducing wastage and the cost of government subsidies (Warwick and Cann 2007; Plan Bleu 2003). Many of these initiatives have made use of local private sector subcontractors under the management and administration of government agencies and local authorities, without resort to private sector finance (see Box 6.1).

While privatization escapes the problems faced by governments in finding the capital for new service infrastructure, it merely transfers the payment of interest on the capital from government to consumers. The poorest consumers cannot afford to pay. A private sector company may, one of the most efficient and equitable utilities in Colombia, if not Latin America, and by 2001, 95 per cent of the population had clean tap water while 87 per cent were connected to the sewerage system, despite the rapidly growing population.

In Savelugu, Ghana, a system has been established whereby water is bought in bulk from the state utility and then the community manages the distribution, maintenance, tariff-setting and collection. Access to potable water has been increased to 74 per cent. The national average for rural areas is 36 per cent.

In Olavanna, India the local community has initiated sixty drinking water schemes, over half of them supported by local government, which are providing reliable water to more than half the local population, in contrast to only about 30 per cent in the 1990s.

In Bangladesh, the government gave the publicly operated employees' cooperative the contract to run the water system in one of Dhaka's zones, with another zone given to a local private company. After the first year's experiment the employees' cooperative results were so good that the Water and Sanitation Authority handed over the private sector's contract to the cooperative.

In Santa Cruz, Bolivia, a cooperative was set up to operate water supply and sewerage; customers now elect the utility's decision-makers. By 1996, water supply had been extended to 272,000 inhabitants and sewerage to 46,700. After achieving these objectives, the cooperative had funds left over that were also used to construct additional sewerage works.

Sources: Balanyá et al. 2005; Hoque 2003; Lobina and Hall 1999; PSIRU 2002 (as summarized in Warwick and Cann 2007)

sometimes, be more efficient than a poorly managed public supply, but even when this is the case the savings may be less than the cost of paying the company's profits. Privatization does not reduce the level of public finance needed for delivering services to the poor, nor obviate the need for government intervention to ensure that they are delivered. Regulation is also needed from an environmental perspective, to ensure that abstraction rates do not deplete aquifers. From an economic perspective strong regulation is essential. Water supply and sewerage services are natural monopolies whether in public or private hands. High-income countries that have privatized them have introduced highly sophisticated regulatory frameworks to minimize the economic inefficiencies of monopoly or oligopoly behaviour. Many developing countries lack the administrative and institutional capacity to do the same.

Many concerns have been expressed over the role of trade liberalization in opening service delivery to international companies (Stevens and Holmes 2005; Higgott and Weber 2005; Chandra 2003). GATS recognizes the right of countries to apply domestic regulations and impose restrictions on trade for 'services provided in the exercise of government authority', provided that such regulations do not constitute 'unnecessary' barriers to trade. In principle liberalization need not undermine the ability of governments to introduce the legislative measures needed to ensure service delivery to the poor. In practice this freedom can be substantially curtailed by ambiguities in interpretation of WTO or regional agreements, asymmetries in political power, lack of transparency in negotiations and institutional deficiencies in domestic politics (Mehta and la Cour Madsen 2005). These problems are compounded by inadequate understanding of a country's regulatory needs at the time commitments are made. The maintenance of sufficient regulatory freedom depends on a country's capacity to specify appropriate limitations in its commitments, which is often lacking. Once a commitment has been made it cannot be withdrawn without renegotiation, which can be extremely costly in terms of concessions required elsewhere.

The privatization of what is essentially a public service and the opening of markets to international companies are not the easy answer that is often assumed to finding the capital investment needed for meeting the Millennium Development Goals. If a developing country with limited regulatory capacity chooses to make liberalization commitments in return for concessions given in other areas of the single undertaking, the cost to its poorest citizens may be considerably greater than it bargained for.

TRANSPORT SERVICES

Liberalization of transport services overlaps with the now defunct WTO negotiations on competition policy. Competition law was put on the WTO agenda at the Singapore ministerial meeting in 1996, and taken off again at Cancún in 2003 when developing countries refused to have anything to do with it. The proposals aimed to eliminate anti-competitive practices in developing countries while doing little to address those still prevalent in high-income ones. A study published in 2002 estimated that price fixing and other cooperative agreements between shipping companies that were either permitted under US and European law or not actively prevented by it raised the cost of international maritime transport by some 24 per cent (Fink et al. 2002). Europe has begun to tackle the issue, but collusive agreements between shipping companies are still partially exempt from anti-trust laws in the USA.

When industrializing Britain was establishing its global trading networks it employed protectionist policies to maximize the profits to British carriers from exporting the manufactured products, importing the raw materials and shipping the necessary labour from Africa. After other countries had adopted similar practices UNCTAD attempted to introduce some degree of order and leave room for the growth of shipping industries in developing countries. Its code of practice allowed 40 per cent of the trade to be reserved for ships belonging to the exporting country, 40 per cent for the importing country and 20 per cent for the rest. Subsequent offshoring of the industry to flags of convenience and the growth of container shipping have reduced the effectiveness of such arrangements, so that agreements between the carriers themselves have become the predominant form of protection. This applies to shipment by air as well as by sea.

Transport services include the provision of infrastructure as well as the carriage of goods. Trade barriers are applied as limits on access of foreign ships or aircraft to domestic ports and airports, on the ownership of facilities for both international and domestic transport, and on the provision of services in them or related to them. Restrictions are imposed in both high-income and low-income countries, often on the grounds of national security. Some degree of public control is needed to avoid monopolistic or oligopolistic behaviour, but there have been highly successful examples of partial privatization and trade liberalization. When Puerto Nuevo in Argentina was opened to both domestic and foreign competition the average charge per container fell by nearly a factor of four. For the world shipping industry as a whole it has been estimated that liberalization of port services would reduce international transport costs by about 9 per cent (ibid.).

It has been argued that liberalization would also have environmental benefits, through the promotion of better management techniques. This is possible, but any such gain would be more than offset by the impacts of increased shipping. This is a separate issue, related to the sustainability of material economic growth as a whole. Putting this wider issue to one side, the liberalization of transport services and the elimination of anti-competitive practices offer considerable economic benefits for all countries, rich and poor. The difficulties of doing it and the means of overcoming them are highly specific to the industry itself. There is nothing to be gained from a country's ports authorities making concessions in return for greater access to foreign markets for its farmers or manufacturers. The inclusion of transport services within the single undertaking of a comprehensive trade agreement serves only to confuse.

BOX 6.2 LIBERALIZATION OF DISTRIBUTION SERVICES IN BRAZIL, KENYA AND MALAYSIA

Dynamics of distribution. In Brazil the concentration of retailing into the hands of a relatively small number of powerful supermarket groups has already gone a long way, particularly in the major cities and more populous regions. There are still many small retailers, but they are under increasing competitive pressure from the bigger outlets. In Kenya the market has not been attractive to larger retailers and most growth has occurred in micro and small distribution enterprises. In Malaysia, which is rapidly industrializing, the most vigorous retail development is in the establishment of larger-scale outlets.

Importance of small outlets. In Brazil companies with fewer than ten employees accounted for 93.5 per cent of retail companies and for 55 per cent of retail employment in 2002, though for only 22 per cent of turnover. In Kenya the sector consists predominantly of micro and small firms, employs a large number of relatively low-skilled workers at low wages, and involves mostly women. In Malaysia small stores employ the majority of workers but larger outlets have gained more ground.

Growth of larger outlets. In Brazil the development of supermarkets started relatively early. The supermarket sector, in which there is a considerable degree of concentration, has long accounted for the greater part of food sales and is the main channel of distribution for basic consumer products. In Kenya supermarkets and other larger-scale outlets are leading to a demand in urban areas for higher service quality, which threatens the smaller retailers. The development of large outlets, however (none of which is foreign owned), slowed during the 1990s because of severe economic conditions and reduced incomes. In Malaysia larger outlets, which are mainly foreign owned, now account for almost 60 per cent of retail sales. This threatens the smaller and family-owned shops, the numbers of which are likely to continue declining, and a standstill has been imposed on hypermarket developments in some areas for environmental reasons.

The general economic environment appears to be the most important factor conditioning the interest of international investors in distribution services. Brazil has a liberal policy towards FDI, but during the economic troubles of the 1980s and early 1990s new investors were deterred, and distribution undertakings already in the market were forced into a process of concentration. In Kenya the liberal policy towards inward investment in distribution has been substantially negated in recent years by the general unattractiveness of the economy to investors and by perceptions of corruption. To this may be added unquantifiable effects arising from strict physical restrictions which are imposed on investments for planning and environmental reasons. In Malaysia, despite a basic investment regime that is much less liberal, and where for social reasons there are requirements for the participation of certain ethnic groups, inward investment in distribution has been so dynamic as to justify the government in restraining it in certain areas.

In both Brazil and Kenya the development of larger distribution outlets could give rise to social effects (especially on employment), and to environmental and resource effects. In Brazil this would merely be as a continuation of the present situation. Kenya already has detailed planning and environmental control laws which, however, need to be more effectively enforced.

Further liberalization in Malaysia would increase the heavy pressure already felt by small retailers and wholesalers. This could increase the need for more highly qualified staff in larger shops, but at the same time reduce employment in smaller firms. Malaysia would have to amend most, or all, of its investment control measures, with possible adverse results for the poorer consumers who benefit from controlled prices and for the smaller food outlets where they shop. The special regulations relating to ethnic participation would probably have to be removed or amended. In the particular ethnic circumstances of Malaysia this could be seen as posing a threat to social stability, which has long been a top priority of the Malaysian government.

Source: Adapted from Arkell and Johnson (2005)

DISTRIBUTION SERVICES

The distribution services of greatest interest to exporters are those provided by the major international supermarket chains. Liberalization gives them significant new opportunities to establish outlets in foreign countries, particularly developing ones, since many developed-country markets are already fairly open. The technological capability of the major companies gives them a competitive advantage over local retailers. As well as giving an economic gain in the parent country through the return on investment, this increases economic efficiency in the importing country. This gives a small increase in economic welfare (economic models typically indicate about 10 per cent of the total from services liberalization), which is the result of big effects on the sector itself. Most of the rise in economic efficiency comes from reducing employment in the industry, with fewer newly created jobs than those lost in small retail outlets (see Box 6.2).

Increased efficiency leads to lower consumer prices for some products, and others are introduced that were not previously available. These benefits apply particularly to higher-income urban consumers, while the employment losses apply to less affluent workers. The introduction of global brands can weaken local cultures and harm local producers. All of these impacts were seen in a study of the effects when retail services were liberalized in Thailand, where they led to major protests and intense political debate (WTO 2002). In Malaysia the expansion of both indigenous and foreign-owned hypermarkets threatened social cohesion and led to a moratorium on further development (Arkell and Johnson 2005). There are significant environmental issues too. The international chains source their products from a much wider area than local suppliers, resulting in more transport, more congestion, more accidents, more pollution, more oil consumption and more climate change. The extra packaging creates extra solid waste.

Liberalization can sometimes provide a platform for the development of competitive local companies using the same technologies as the multinationals. It comes at a cost that may not be worth paying.

OVERALL IMPACT ON SUSTAINABLE DEVELOPMENT

As with manufacturing and agriculture, the economic benefits that have traditionally been claimed for services trade liberalization are overstated. They may be somewhat bigger than for trade in goods, but still not big enough to make a significant difference. For some services there are potential benefits for developing countries, but they come from dynamic effects and not from economic efficiency gains.

For many service industries, such as construction, energy, business, education, health, cultural, sporting and tourism, the stakes are fairly low. Telecommunication and transport services offer significant benefits for their own sake, with no need to bargain over them in the single undertakings of the WTO and other trade agreements. Most countries stand to gain from opening their markets to international competition in both, but being offered a carrot in some other area is not a good reason for doing it.

For liberalization of distribution services the more affluent sections of society in developing countries tend to gain while the poorer ones lose. The environment loses. There can be some environmental benefits from liberalizing environmental services, but the provision of affordable safe water and sanitation to poor communities is more likely to get worse than better. Ready access to efficient financial services is a key factor in improving the performance of the whole economy in any country, but most would do better to strengthen their own provision than rely on the competence of foreign suppliers and hand them the interest on the loans. The impact of financial services liberalization has on many occasions in the past been disastrous. The benefits it offers to developing countries are disturbingly similar to those which high-income countries hoped to reap themselves from the financial systems that collapsed in chaos in 2008.

Europe's vision of a globally sustainable future as set out in its Lisbon strategy is one in which Europe earns its invisible income as the world's supplier of high technology, high finance and other high-value services, while other countries carry on supplying the commodities and the low-added-value goods. America's vision is more self-reliant but not by much. It is not a strategy that promotes the development of poor countries. Some aspects of it positively inhibit development, harm the environment as much as they help, or take major risks with financial and economic stability. The liberalization of some services can contribute to sustainable development, but the agenda as a whole has the opposite effect.

7 | TRIPS ABROAD

For knowledge itself is power. (Bacon 1597)

Intellectual property rights such as patents and copyright protection are intended to stimulate innovation, at the cost of restricting competition. In developing national legislation governments aim for an optimal balance. International protection is provided through the WTO agreement on Trade-Related aspects of Intellectual Property Rights (TRIPs) and its extensions in regional and bilateral trade agreements.

In this chapter we examine the likely impacts for each of the main aspects. The original TRIPs agreement had an adverse effect on public health in low-income countries, which has been at least partly countered by its subsequent amendment. Extension of the provisions for protection of geographical product names would have a fairly small overall effect, with a benefit to European and other suppliers and losses to their competitors. Intellectual property rights for genetic materials have social effects that are generally negative, with high environmental risks that are insufficiently constrained by global environmental agreements. The biggest effects are those related to industrial development. International protection benefits countries whose level of technological development is already high, at the cost of limiting the ability of developing countries to develop.

INTELLECTUAL PROPERTY

Combining the words 'biological' and 'piracy' to make a new word, 'biopiracy', is a clever device for making the reader think it immoral to gather genetic material in a foreign country, analyse it, describe it and earn a profit from its commercial use. Equally ingenious is the idea of combining the two unrelated words 'intellectual' and 'property' to make a new phrase, 'intellectual property'. It sows in the reader's mind the irrational belief that whoever thinks of such an idea first somehow 'owns' it, and that anyone who then uses it has 'stolen' it. In reality my use of the clever new word and the ingenious new phrase takes nothing away from anyone, so cannot possibly be theft. There is no sense in which the people who first thought of them can own them, unless a government were to pass a law saying they do. The same applies to a scientific description of genetic material, and to any other knowledge or idea. Its 'ownership' is a purely legal construct.

If someone were to publish this book in his or her own name the author might, if so moved, sue them for fraud. He would have no need of copyright law, which serves a different purpose. When copyright protection was first introduced it was granted not to authors but to publishers, to stop anyone else producing the book and diminishing their sales. For other types of product 'letters patent' were used by the kings and queens of England to grant monopoly rights to favoured companies in return for a share of the inflated profits (Seth 2004). When mounting opposition led to the practice being curtailed in the early seventeenth century an exception was made for new inventions, to encourage innovation. Subsequent patent laws allowed monopoly rights to be granted only for such products, and only for a limited period after their introduction.

The inclusion of copyright, patents and other intellectual property rights (IPR) in trade agreements is the opposite of all other aspects of the trade liberalization agenda. Instead of promoting competition it inhibits it. The monopoly rights granted through such legislation stop anyone competing with whoever introduces a new idea first, until whoever writes the rules thinks they should.

As well as patents for new inventions and copyright for literary and artistic works (and now computer software), the legal concept of intellectual property covers trade secrets, trademarks, the aesthetic aspects of industrial designs, geographical product names like Champagne and specific (*sui generis*) systems applicable to activities that are not easily patented. The last of these includes rights for plant breeders and designers of electronic integrated circuits. National IPR legislation aims to improve the performance of an economy by giving companies or individuals monopoly rights in any or all of these areas.

A country's economy may benefit in two main ways. First, the extra profits from a monopoly enable bigger investments to be made in research and development and the production facilities for new products, and may therefore contribute to economic growth. Similar considerations apply to marketing expenditure for promoting musical productions, brand names and non-patentable designs. Second, patent laws require the details of inventions to be disclosed, helping other inventors make incremental improvements. The duration of the monopoly is chosen so as to strike what is considered to be an optimal balance between inhibiting competition and stimulating innovation. Legislation aims to maximize the performance of the economy to which it applies. Innovators have no protection against foreign competitors unless other governments pass similar laws and make agreements for mutual recognition.

When the USA introduced its widely respected patent laws they required an invention to be an original idea globally and not just in the USA. Patents were granted only to US citizens, however, who remained free to copy foreign designs. When rights were subsequently extended to foreigners they were subject to much higher fees. It was not until the late nineteenth century that countries that had reached similar levels of industrialization expected to gain more than they would lose from granting each other's inventors equal treatment to their own (Khan 2008). International treaties began to proliferate, but considerable variations in IPR laws remained. As the global economy became more integrated the escalating cost of developing products for global markets led to increasing pressure for global protection. The World Intellectual Property Organization (WIPO) was established in 1970 to promote the protection of IPR throughout the world. As a UN organization WIPO gives equal voting rights to all its members, and developing countries had little difficulty in blocking proposals requiring them to give rights to foreign companies. The goal was then pursued through the separate framework of trade agreements, enabling pressure to be applied through trade sanctions.

In the Uruguay Round the USA, Europe, Japan and other industrialized countries united in pressing for the inclusion of IPR while developing countries were still focusing their limited negotiating resources on opposing the GATS proposals (J. P. Singh 2006). The initial opposition to the inclusion of IPR was divided by threats of unilateral sanctions against any country that blocked the proposals and offers of concessions in other areas of the single undertaking. Arguments over counterfeiting and the interests of the pharmaceutical industry led to limited concessions on pharmaceuticals while diverting attention from the wider issues. When the USA passed new domestic legislation strengthening its ability to impose sanctions the opposition petered out.

Once the Uruguay Round's agreement on Trade-Related aspects of Intellectual Property Rights (TRIPs) had been signed concerns over its impacts in developing countries began to grow. The effects on public health received particular attention and became a major issue at Seattle and subsequently in the preparations for the Doha conference. The involvement of NGOs and the mass media enabled a coalition of developing countries to outmanoeuvre the international pharmaceutical companies by reframing the issue as a barrier to the treatment of AIDs (Odell and Sell 2006). This had little influence on US negotiators but the EU softened its position. At Doha it was agreed to review TRIPs specifically in relation to public health. Other aspects of the Doha agenda aimed to strengthen the TRIPs requirements rather than relax them. In parallel the USA and the EU have continued to pursue TRIPs-plus commitments through regional and bilateral agreements.

TRIPs and its proposed amendments affect four main issues: public health, the use of geographical product names, industrial development policy and biological diversity. Each of these is discussed separately below. As noted in Chapter 3, economic models are not capable of modelling these types of measure with any confidence, and the assessment of impacts was based mainly on qualitative considerations and the findings of the research literature.

TRIPS AND PUBLIC HEALTH

The main health concern expressed at Doha related to TRIPs provisions that prevented the export of low-cost generic versions of patented medicines to countries without the capacity to make them. This includes treatments for diseases such as tuberculosis, malaria, pneumonia, meningitis and diarrhoea, as well as HIV/AIDS and other sexually transmitted diseases. TRIPs required producing countries such as India to pay royalties to the patent holder, but left them free to manufacture the medicines under a compulsory licence without needing the patent holder's permission, but only for their own public health use, notably in cases of national emergency. The Doha conference recognized the problem faced by smaller developing countries, and in 2003 a waiver was introduced allowing the export of generic drugs in cases of need. In 2005 an amendment to TRIPs was approved that would replace the waiver once it was accepted by the WTO membership.

The change has had little direct effect (Haakonsson and Richey 2007). Little use has been made of the provisions for export under compulsory licensing, whose procedures have been argued to be unworkable (Oxfam 2005). Some countries have instead set up their own manufacturing facilities, often with foreign assistance. Others that are highly dependent on donor financing have continued to buy medicines from the patent holders, usually at reduced prices. It is possible that these price reductions might have been given voluntarily, but there was a strong incentive from the threat of the TRIPs amendment. The amendment may therefore have had a significant indirect impact on keeping the price of medicines down. In some cases the full price of patented drugs is well over a factor of ten higher than that of the corresponding generics (Oxfam 2002a, 2002b). Instances have been reported where the number of patients receiving HIV/AIDS therapy was tripled by taking advantage of the lower prices (Mishra 2002).

Such figures give only a rough indication of possible effects and cannot be used as a measure of the total number of patients benefiting. The actual delivery of therapy depends on the human, physical and financial resourcing of health services as well as the price of drugs. Nevertheless, the amendment may have had a significant beneficial impact on public health, through at least partly countering a significantly adverse one from the original TRIPs agreement.

The main argument put forward by pharmaceutical companies against relaxing the original agreement was that it would constrain their R&D expenditure for new drugs. This, however, does not stand up to closer scrutiny. It has been estimated that the difference in income for OECD companies would have been less than $1 billion (Abbott 2002). This would not be a loss of income, but the absence of the extra income arising from an agreement that allowed them to expand their sales of patented drugs. Their total R&D expenditure is about $22 billion. This is a small proportion of total R&D spending on new drugs, most of which is for research in universities and research institutes funded by the public sector or charitable organizations. Most of it is devoted to developing drugs for high-income countries' markets, not for the different needs of low-income ones. The same would have applied to the extra $1 billion. Any influence on public health in developed countries would be small, while in developing ones it would be too small to be significant. The only significant adverse impact of relaxing the TRIPs requirement is likely to have been the absence of a small increase in the profitability of the major pharmaceutical companies and a correspondingly small effect on their countries' economies.

GEOGRAPHICAL PRODUCT NAMES

The original TRIPs agreement included general provisions for the protection of product names associated with particular geographical locations. The Doha agenda aimed to strengthen these provisions through a multilateral system for registering specific names, initially for wines and spirits and subsequently for other products. The proposals were promoted by the EU and other countries with a large heritage of recognized names, and opposed by those whose industries compete with their products.

It has been argued that the inclusion of products other than wines and spirits would be appropriate for protecting traditional knowledge in developing countries, since other types of IPR do not easily accommodate collective ownership. It is extraordinarily difficult, however, to establish rights to traditional knowledge by any means, and the potential benefits may not be attainable in countries with limited ability to invest in the marketing and advertising needed to establish a brand image. In such circumstances a name may gain greater market exposure without protection (McCalman 2002).

The restrictions on competition from the proposed extension to TRIPs would increase profits in protected countries through a rise in prices in consuming ones. The EU would be the biggest beneficiary, with corresponding losses elsewhere. The net effect on global economic welfare would be negative but small.

TRIPS AND INDUSTRIAL DEVELOPMENT

Examples abound of how some of the most successful global companies began business by copying innovations made by their foreign competitors. America's industrial development started by copying designs for textile machinery patented in England but not in the USA (Dutfield 2004). The origins of Unilever's global food business were in the production of margarine using processes invented in France but not patented in Holland (Moser 2003). The Dutch lighting and electronics giant Philips was founded on copying the designs for light bulbs patented by Thomas Edison in the USA, and before then by Joseph Swan in England. The Swedish telecommunications company Ericsson made free use of the inventions of Alexander Graham Bell. Much of the Japanese semiconductor industry was founded on American designs for which the Japanese Patent Office was slow in granting patents. Firms in the newly industrialized countries of East Asia were positively encouraged to circumvent other countries' patents. As we saw in Chapter 4, this contributed to a dramatic development success story that predated TRIPs.

TRIPs goes beyond previous international agreements to require all WTO members to recognize a minimum set of worldwide rules for intellectual property rights. It also extends the coverage of IPR recognition, in some cases into areas not even included in some industrial countries' own legislation (Watal 2002). Developing countries were given until January 2000 to comply, and the least developed ones until 2006 (with longer grace periods for pharmaceutical products). It was not envisaged that these countries would have succeeded in industrial development by then. The aim was only to give them time to introduce the necessary legislation and administrative systems to comply with the new rules.

In support of its stance the European Commission argues that TRIPs is an essential tool for developing countries to attract foreign investment, to promote technology transfer and to protect their own rights holders (European Commission 2005b). None of these arguments stands up to scrutiny. TRIPs may have a positive influence on FDI, but FDI has only a limited beneficial impact on development and may have an adverse one.[14] Technology is transferred far more easily by copying a design than by granting monopoly rights to its inventor, as is clearly demonstrated by the development successes that predate TRIPs. Local rights holders have no need of international protection until they have developed the technological capability to compete internationally. Once that point is reached a developing country will need to join international IPR agreements for its own economic benefit. Being forced to do so prematurely through the single undertaking of a trade agreement hampers its development in order to benefit competing countries that have already industrialized.

Just as TRIPs is the opposite of the other components of the trade liberalization agenda in restricting competition instead of promoting it, the main economic argument in its favour is also the opposite. The traditional case for removing tariffs and other trade barriers is based on static economic efficiency and ignores the dynamic effects. The economic case for TRIPs is based on dynamic efficiency and ignores the static ones. Its restrictions on competition aim to promote technical change and the long-term growth of the global economy, from which all countries are presumed to benefit. Since the vast majority of patents are held by companies and individuals in industrialized countries, however, the agreement promotes the dynamic efficiency of developed countries rather than developing ones (Singh and Dhumale 1999). The short-term static impact is a transfer of income from poor countries to rich ones, while the long-term dynamic effect on global growth gives no more than a marginal benefit to the poor ones (Hoekman and Holmes 1999; McCalman 2005). The dynamic effect on a developing country's own self-generated growth can be large and negative.

With TRIPs now in place industrialized countries can claim strong grounds for seeking more rigorous enforcement. What they aim to enforce is an agreement that limits developing countries' ability to develop in the same way as they did themselves. Regional and bilateral negotiations aim for yet tighter restrictions that make industrial development even harder (Shadlen 2005).

TRIPS AND BIOLOGICAL DIVERSITY

'How can you buy or sell the sky, the warmth of the land?' Many environmentalists are familiar with those words, often attributed to

North American Indian Chief Seattle when signing the treaty that ended the Indian Wars. They were written by screenwriter Ted Perry, imagining what the chief might have asked as he contemplated the sale of the Indian lands (Zussy 1993). Had either of them seen TRIPs coming they might have asked the same of the very essence of life. TRIPs provides the stake-posts for laying claim to ownership of the design of living organisms, whether they be designed by genetic engineering, traditional breeding, evolution by natural selection or divine creation. In a world that believes in buying and selling anything whose boundaries can be staked out, the ethical considerations play little part. Most of the controversy revolves around the economics, the politics and, to a lesser degree, the ecological risk.

The TRIPs agreement requires governments to grant IPR protection for micro-organisms, microbiological processes and plant varieties. For plant varieties purpose-designed (*sui generis*) regimes may be used as an alternative to patents, but the other two must be patentable. In principle only new inventions can be protected, but North American and European patent law treats discoveries of natural substances as though they were inventions (Dutfield 2002). The discovery by modern science of what has been known to traditional farmers or indigenous peoples for many hundreds or thousands of years allows property rights to be claimed by the first company or individual to create a formal record of it. Life-forms cannot be patented in their natural state, but they can be when made available for industrial use for the first time.

The economic argument in favour is the same as for industrial products, with the same weaknesses. It may also be claimed that when a product has medicinal or agricultural use its commercialization will help to cure the world's sick or feed its poor. Neither argument is well substantiated. As we saw with TRIPs and public health, private sector pharmaceutical research tends to be directed towards curing the rich world's sick and not the poor world's. As we saw with agricultural liberalization, traditional agriculture and publicly funded research have been considerably more successful than agribusiness in reducing world poverty.

The political and ecological arguments relate to the relationship between TRIPs and the UN Earth Summit's Convention on Biological Diversity (CBD). They are mainly political. Between the completion of the Uruguay Round and the meeting in Doha much of the opposition to TRIPs focused on a potential conflict with the CBD. The Doha meeting took note of the debate and set up ongoing discussions. The CBD has three objectives: the conservation of biological diversity; the sustainable use of its components; and the fair and equitable sharing of the benefits from the use of genetic resources. The last of these is the main focus of debate, both in the WTO and in the implementation of the CBD (Straus 2008). The negotiations revolve around the respective claims to monopoly rights of corporations, sovereign states and traditional communities. The ecological concerns raised by scientists and NGOs take a back seat.

Some 90 per cent of the world's genetic material of potential value to agribusiness and pharmaceutical companies is in the natural habitats of developing countries. Only 10 per cent has survived the agricultural and industrial development of the developed ones. In both the WTO and regional negotiations the industrialized countries aim to extend those TRIPs provisions which give rights for the use of this material to their companies. The developing ones aim for amendments that would favour theirs.

The main goals of the USA and the EU are universal adoption of the 1991 guidelines of the international Union for the Protection of New Varieties of Plants (UPOV), and the Budapest Treaty on the International Recognition of the Deposit of Micro-organisms. These clarify the TRIPs requirement for 'effective' *sui generis* protection, and simplify the process of getting patents in multiple countries (GRAIN 2005; Khor 2007). The word 'effective' then means compliance with UPOV. Countries lose the freedom to define their own *sui generis* systems to meet their own needs. Both UPOV and the Budapest treaty were developed in response to pressure from Western companies. Their adoption presents difficulties for developing countries, both in their capacity to introduce them and the costs of regulating them (Rangnekar 2002). Biodiversity-rich developing countries oppose them. They aim instead for mandatory requirements to disclose the origin of genetic resources and proof that consent has been given for their use (CEAS 2000). This would enable preferential treatment to be given to their companies. In theory it might also enable the granting of legal and commercial rights to traditional communities.

Indigenous peoples are most unlikely to see any benefit from either set of proposals. Commercial rights are totally inconsistent with their lifestyles, while the only legal right of any value to them is exclusive access to their own lands. The main impacts on traditional communities are those affecting small farmers.

It has been argued that if the origin of genetic materials had to be disclosed this would protect the traditional knowledge of farming communities. It is doubtful whether any such arrangement would be legally enforceable (European Commission 2002b; CIPR 2002). Meanwhile, studies on the effects of introducing plant variety protection indicate no clear evidence that protection has led to an overall increase in R&D activity, either in the USA or in middle-income developing countries (CIPR 2002). Commercial farmers and the seed industry are seen as the main beneficiaries, while poor farmers see little direct benefit and experience restrictions on seed saving and exchange. The new seed varieties generally offer a commercial advantage to the large farms that buy them. This can result in reduced availability and increased cost of traditional varieties that would otherwise be more profitable for small farmers. Increasing dependence on seed retention can lead to falling quality and declining yields, leaving no alternative but to adopt the new varieties. All agricultural output then becomes dependent on a small number of varieties, supplied by a small number of major corporations, with legal barriers to seed saving and exchange.

New plant varieties can increase agricultural productivity, but the evidence is mixed on whether this reduces poverty or pressure on natural habitats (Scoones 2002). Developments related to transgenic crops generate major concerns over ecosystem stability that cannot yet be evaluated with any certainty. Assessing the validity of these concerns and identifying other issues of potential concern are hampered by an exceptionally small core of scientific information (Batie and Ervin 2001). Evidence to date is limited even for the potential environmental benefits that certain varieties are designed to achieve.

In these circumstances it is impossible to assess the biodiversity impact of TRIPs with any precision, beyond the observation that the claims are poorly substantiated, the risks are high and the associated social impacts are generally negative. Conservation of biological diversity revolves primarily around protecting habitats, to which intellectual property rights make no real contribution (CEAS 2000). It would be wrong to blame the WTO for this unsatisfactory state of affairs, or the trade officials who negotiate in it, or those who develop regional trade agreements. They are not biologists or ecologists. The fault lies with the CBD. It has allowed itself to become embroiled in economics and politics at the expense of its principal task, to conserve biological diversity. Only the CBD can develop the necessary international law, which has to be sufficiently precise to place binding constraints on the WTO and everyone else.

OVERALL IMPACT ON SUSTAINABLE DEVELOPMENT

The adverse effect on public health in low-income countries of the original TRIPs agreement has been at least partly countered by its subsequent amendment. The overall effect of the agreement, however, has been to benefit countries whose level of technological development is already high, at the cost of limiting the ability of low-income ones to develop. The granting of property rights for genetic materials has social effects that are generally negative, with environmental risks that are high and insufficiently constrained by global environmental agreements. The overall impact of TRIPs on sustainable development is significantly negative. The TRIPs-plus provisions in preferential trade agreements make the adverse effects even bigger.

8 | FILLING THE GAPS

I have never known much good done by those who affected to trade
for the public good. It is an affectation, indeed, not very common
among merchants, and very few words need be employed in dissuad-
ing them from it. (Smith 1904 [1776]: 360)

The Uruguay Round that was completed in 1994 went a long way
towards eliminating tariffs on non-agricultural goods, but many other
barriers were left in place. At the 1996 WTO meeting in Singapore
four new items were put on the agenda. These covered trade facilitation, government procurement, competition and investment. These
'Singapore issues' aimed to fill the remaining gaps in market opening
for industrial exports and capital. Many developing-country representatives were suspicious. Following the deadlock in Seattle they agreed in
Doha that negotiations on the new issues could begin after the Cancún
conference in 2003, but only if an explicit consensus were achieved on
their modalities. As clarified by the chairman in the closing session at
Doha, negotiations would not proceed unless every WTO member were
prepared to join in that consensus. Only trade facilitation survived. In
Cancún a coalition of developing countries blocked the other three.
They have not entirely disappeared. They remain on the back burner
in the WTO agenda, and are actively pursued by the EU and the USA
in regional and bilateral agreements.

This chapter examines the impacts of proposed agreements for each
of the four Singapore issues. The provisions for trade facilitation can
make a positive contribution to economic development, but the effect
is small. Those on government procurement would give a small short-
term benefit, but at the cost of impairing developing countries' ability to
employ simple and effective policy tools for their long-term development.
The impacts of the proposals on competition policy are similar. Those for
investment promote the interests of investors over those of the countries
they invest in, and prohibit a wide range of measures that have made a
major contribution to some of the biggest development successes.

TRADE FACILITATION

The aim of trade facilitation is to reduce or eliminate the costs and
bureaucratic hurdles that exporters or importers face in getting their

products through a country's borders even when tariffs have been removed. The consensus that was achieved in Cancún reflects a broad agreement among developing as well as developed countries that it can offer significant economic benefits to both. The costs of trade would fall, the volume of trade would rise, and developing countries would get an extra benefit from more efficient collection of whatever tariff revenues they are still allowed to gather. The negotiations revolve mainly around the extent to which these countries are prepared to commit themselves to actions they would not take of their own accord, and the level of financial support that developed countries are prepared to give.

That is not the whole story. The World Bank's performance reviews reveal large variations between developed countries, many of which perform worse than many developing ones on some of the key indicators (Arvis et al 2007; World Bank 2008). Logistics costs in several EU countries are higher than in much of Asia and Latin America. Argentina requires fewer import documents than Spain. The direct costs of importing into Brazil are lower than for the UK. Most high-income countries apply technical and health standards that developing ones regard as barriers to trade (see Box 8.1). The commitments sought in trade negotiations therefore go in both directions. Nevertheless, the transaction costs and bureaucratic hurdles are on average higher in developing countries than in developed ones, and most of the pressure is on developing ones to reform their systems. Few are prepared to go beyond what they are already doing unless they are paid for it.

The proposed reform measures cover computerization, the logistics of moving goods through ports, the preparation and transfer of documents, the cost, complexity, transparency and professionalism of customs and regulatory procedures, and the harmonization of systems and standards. The World Customs Organization (WCO) has established a code of good practice in the International Convention on the Simplification and Harmonization of Customs Procedures (the Kyoto Convention). Many developing countries have not signed up to it. Constraints on achieving the required standards include inflexible institutions, lack of modern communications and information systems and inadequately skilled staff (Hoekman 2001).

It is impossible to eliminate all the costs of importing and exporting without completely removing border controls. Many estimates have been made of how much the costs might be reduced, typically by comparing the average performance in developing countries with that in developed ones. When these estimates are fed into economic models the results seem to be dramatic, with numbers that can be as big as or bigger than

---

**BOX 8.1 PERCEIVED TECHNICAL BARRIERS TO TRADE
FOR IMPORTING INTO THE EU**

In a stakeholder survey conducted as part of the SIA study for the proposed EU–Mercosur trade agreement, the new EU regulations on Registration, Valuation, Authorization and Restriction of Chemicals (REACH) were identified as one of the main concerns for importing into the EU for interviewees in all three countries surveyed (Argentina, Brazil and Uruguay). They have been the subject of major concern in Chambers of Exporters and Chemical Chambers in Argentina and Brazil.

REACH is a complex system of registration that covers not only chemicals but also chemical derivatives. It affects exports of many other products, including footwear, textiles, leather goods, household appliances, pharmaceuticals, food additives, animal nutrition products, cosmetics, fuels and minerals, as well as chemical products. The costs of registration are at present uncertain but are expected to be high, and particularly onerous for SMEs. Exporters and government officials consulted considered REACH to be a strong technical barrier to trade.

The government of Argentina has submitted a Communication to the WTO expressing serious concern over inadequacies in Europe's registration systems for foreign suppliers, including the provision of information and technical assistance through the WTO enquiry point and the European Chemicals Agency. The Communication considers that the current arrangements constitute a serious impediment to the continued presence of foreign companies in the European market, particularly SMEs.

Source: Derived from Estudio López Dardaine (2009)

---

those from completely eliminating all tariffs. For the Doha negotiations most models indicate that the global welfare gain would be larger than that for agricultural and non-agricultural tariff reductions combined. As we have already seen, economic welfare gains of this magnitude are considerably less significant than is often claimed. The effect on the volume of international trade, however, and the associated increases and decreases in production, would be very significant indeed. If they really were as big as the models predict, they too would be as big as or bigger than those from tariff reductions. The same applies to all the consequent impacts on people and the environment. If the economic benefits really were big, the social and environmental impacts would be even bigger.

In reality it is most unlikely that any of the impacts would be anything like that significant. Most developing countries that cannot afford to computerize their customs procedures have already received assistance for doing it, from the World Bank and other development agencies. Similar assistance has been provided for other trade facilitation measures, some effective, some not. Most other reforms are harder to implement, with bigger difficulties in ensuring that development assistance actually works. When developing countries negotiate trade facilitation measures in trade agreements they have been extremely careful not to commit to anything they would not do anyway with whatever additional assistance they might need, or to agree to penalties for failing to deliver. Any extra funding made available through a trade agreement would be useful, but cannot realistically be expected to make more than a minor difference to the efforts that are already being made on a difficult task. Claims that the trade facilitation measures in trade agreements offer huge benefits, or huge costs, attempt to make a lot out of little.

GOVERNMENT PROCUREMENT

The proposed measures on government procurement aim to open a large market that would otherwise be exempt from free trade. Government spending on private sector goods and services is often restricted to national suppliers, and other countries' exporters would dearly like to gain access to it. It averages about 8 per cent of GDP in OECD countries and 5 per cent in developing ones (OECD 2002). Reasons for discrimination in favour of domestic suppliers include avoiding the cost of international tendering procedures, maintaining control over macroeconomic or development policy, promoting the development of particular industries or regions, and maintaining national security. America's discriminatory investment in its space programme is widely considered to have paid off handsomely in the global lead it gave to its microelectronics and computing industries.

Since the late 1970s market-oriented policies in OECD countries have led to a greater degree of liberalization. The Uruguay Round included a Government Procurement Agreement (GPA) defining procedures and thresholds for international tendering, with provisions for transparency and avoiding the use of technical barriers to trade. The GPA binds only its signatories, and most developing countries have not joined. Initial proposals for the 1996 Singapore conference aimed to extend the GPA to bind all WTO members, but the goal was subsequently narrowed to focus on the issue of transparency (Khor 1997). At Doha the agenda for government procurement was confined to the transparency issue, with the explicit statement that negotiations would not restrict the scope for countries to give preferences to domestic suppliers.

In recognizing the case for a multilateral agreement on transparency the Doha Declaration made no attempt to explain what that case was. Since the proposed agreement would not restrict countries' ability to discriminate in favour of domestic suppliers, it is not clear that the issue is relevant to trade. At Singapore the US stated the aim of reducing corruption (ibid.). This is not a trade issue, particularly if procurement can still be restricted to domestic suppliers. In rejecting the Doha proposals at Cancún one of the main concerns of developing countries was to avoid what they saw as a first step towards banning domestic preferences (Das 2002).

If an agreement on government procurement were restricted to the transparency issue the impacts would be small. The necessary procedures would be a WTO requirement rather than a national initiative, and would probably be applied only to those purchasing decisions that are likely to be challenged by foreign companies. This would tend to reduce domestic corruption for such contracts, but may also make purchasing authorities more susceptible to lobbying pressure and associated incentives from transnational corporations. The overall impact is likely to be downward pressure on prices for at least some of these contracts, but there is little evidence on how big the effect might be. The proportion of contracts affected would probably be small, and possibly zero, since preferential treatment would remain legitimate even when a foreign bidder offered a lower price.

The goals of the EU and the USA in regional and bilateral negotiations are not limited to transparency. One of the eight key components of the EU's trade strategy is to eliminate 'restrictive public procurement practices which discriminate against EU suppliers' (European Commission 2006b: 11). The potential economic impacts are bigger than for transparency, but difficult to quantify. Even within Europe's own single market very few public contracts are awarded directly to suppliers in other member states, although successful tendering through a subsidiary in the purchasing country is common (UNDP 2003: ch. 15). Very little research has been done into the effect on prices. A review by the EC concludes that for some products they may be nearly 30 per cent lower for procurement by open tender than for direct contracts (European Commission 2004b). This gives little indication of the influence of cross-border trade, however. Even for trade within a single member state the observed price difference is due at least in part to differences between those contracts which require open tendering under EU legislation and those which do not. Even less research has been done into the impacts of initiatives in developing countries. From a review of the literature Simon Evenett and Bernard Hoekman conclude that while much is claimed for the benefits of making binding commitments to procurement reforms, the evidence is insufficient to make a convincing case (Evenett and Hoekman 2005).

Competitive tendering can be cumbersome and expensive. Even high-income countries do not apply it to all public sector purchases. Many developing countries could make greater use of open tenders, including from foreign suppliers, and for some types of contract the savings would probably outweigh the procedural costs. Failure to take advantage of such savings is not necessarily an indication of corrupt practices. Even when it is, the actions needed to counter corruption are considerably wider and deeper than can be achieved through a trade agreement.

More generally, preferential treatment for domestic suppliers can be a simple and effective policy tool for economic management and long-term development strategy. Decisions on when foreign suppliers should and should not be used are a matter for a country's own government, affecting issues that lie well beyond the expertise of its trade officials. The long-term cost of making binding commitments in a trade agreement could be far greater than the short-term savings, and far outweigh whatever the country's trade negotiators might be offered in return.

COMPETITION

The proposed competition measures aim to harmonize all countries' laws and policies on anti-competitive practices. The Singapore proposal was the second of two attempts in the past few decades to achieve a binding international agreement on competition policy. The first was the UN initiative of 1980 on Equitable Principles and Rules for the Control of Restrictive Practices. This aimed to protect countries' economies from anti-competitive practices by transnational corporations. Binding commitments were sought by developing countries and rejected by industrial ones (UNDP 2003: ch. 14). The subsequent WTO initiative proposed at Singapore was the opposite, promoted by industrial countries and rejected by developing ones. Its objectives are not the same as those of the earlier UN initiative. One of its main proponents is the EU, whose declared trade strategy is to 'ensure European firms do not suffer in third countries from unreasonable subsidization of local companies or anti-competitive practices' (European Commission 2006b: 7). The objectives of the UN initiative (to restrict the practices of transnational corporations), and those of the WTO one (to restrict those of developing countries' governments and firms), are not necessarily inconsistent. The extent to which either is achieved would depend on the details of an agreement.

Few developing countries had any great need for competition laws and policies until they started privatizing their industries in the late 1980s and 1990s. Since then many countries have already introduced them, with provisions designed for the needs of a developing country, not the more complex requirements of a developed one. It took the USA seven years to develop the capability to enforce the price-fixing provisions of its Sherman Act, eleven before the UK could enforce its ban on cartels, twelve for the cartel provisions in the EU's Treaty of Rome, and twenty for the amended cartel law in Japan (A. Singh 2004). Countries with smaller government budgets and fewer professional staff in their enforcement agencies are unlikely to develop similar capabilities any faster, if at all, whether given technical assistance or not.

Competition policy can be used to restrict or prohibit government subsidies and other forms of support, or to contain the anti-competitive practices of private firms. As well as cartels, these include other forms of collusion, predatory pricing (where the market leader raises its prices after cutting them to drive out the competition) and the use of mergers and acquisitions to eliminate competitors. Different countries deal with them differently. US anti-trust law has moved away from a standardized approach towards case-by-case examination of the needs of individual industries (UNDP 2003: ch. 14). Laws and policies in the EU also treat different economic sectors differently, while the harmonization of EU law tends to focus on static efficiency with a lack of clarity in its treatment of state aid. Japanese law has evolved in parallel with its industrial development, with policies that positively favoured cartels and other cooperation between nominal competitors during its period of rapid economic growth. Many developing countries have similarly targeted their competition policies towards their own specific needs, aiming to optimize competitive conditions for state intervention and their own national firms. National competition policy is limited in its ability to challenge the anti-competitive behaviour of transnational corporations. It can do little to stop other countries' anti-dumping actions, with evidence that these have been used as a straightforward protectionist device. It has been estimated that if US anti-dumping cases had been subject to standards equivalent to those of its own competition policy, over 90 per cent of them would have failed (Singh and Dhumale 1999).

Little information is available on the economic impact of anti-competitive practices in developing countries, since most of the legal actions have been against those based in OECD ones. Estimates of the effect that various cartels have had on prices range from about 10 per cent to 100 per cent (Levenstein et al. 2003). As well as the costs to consumers in the producing country there can be adverse impacts on both consumers and producers in the countries to which they export. It has been estimated that the value of international trade affected by cartels based in OECD countries could be as high as 12 per cent of developing-country imports and 2.8 per cent of their GDP. The ability of developing countries to seek redress is limited. Competition law in the USA and other OECD countries focuses on the damage to their own consumers and economies, not those of foreign countries.

Efforts to contain the anti-competitive practices of transnational corporations depend mainly on competition laws in the USA, the EU and other high-income countries. International cooperation is pursued through the OECD. The WTO agenda and other trade agreements have different aims, to contain the anti-competitive practices of companies and governments in developing countries. By the time the Doha proposals were rejected at Cancún the EU had made concessions that reduced the proposed agreement to two main requirements: a ban on 'hard core' cartels, and compliance with the WTO core principles of national treatment and the most favoured nation rule. Both are problematic.

Banning anything so obviously distasteful as a hard-core cartel would be universally applauded if anyone knew what it was. Ajit Singh calls them 'odious by definition' (Singh 2004: 14). OECD countries have settled on their own definition, which is sufficiently imprecise to embrace all their different laws and remains open to different interpretations by different jurisdictions (International Competition Network 2005). Almost any anti-competitive practice can be excluded, with the proviso that 'all exclusions and authorisations of what would otherwise be hard core cartels should be transparent and should be reviewed periodically to assess whether they are both necessary and no broader than necessary to achieve their overriding policy objectives' (OECD 1998). If this were incorporated into a trade agreement it would give the WTO, or, for bilateral agreements, trade officials in the USA or the EU, the authority to tell another country what it must do in order to achieve its own policy objectives, and bar it from doing anything else.

The problems with the WTO core principles are similar. National treatment and the most favoured nation rule are provisions for market access, not for industrial development. If they were applied to competition policy they would stop a country encouraging mergers between its own companies in order to gain the necessary economies of scale for competing with transnational corporations, unless equal encouragement were given to the transnationals to take them over (Singh and Dhumale 1999). If the same principles were applied to EU development policy, all contracts funded from the European Commission's research and development budget would be banned, as would those of member states, unless equal contracts were placed with every foreign competitor. The same logic would require the same for much of the US defence budget. Applying the WTO core principles to the competition policies of developing countries would stop them implementing similar development strategies to those used by developed ones in their own development, with long-term adverse consequences far greater than any possible efficiency gains.

There is a strong economic case for any country to strengthen its own national competition policy, tailored to its own particular economic and developmental needs. There is an equally strong case for the OECD countries to take international action to control the international practices of international corporations, with whatever assistance they might need from developing countries. The only case for developing countries to make binding commitments within the single undertaking of a trade agreement is the hope of gaining from whatever might be offered in return. The attempt to persuade them to make such commitments is a raw market access agenda dressed up in the scantiest of economic clothes.

INVESTMENT

The proposed investment measures would extend investor rights and freedom of capital ownership beyond the provision of banking and other financial services to include the establishment and acquisition of private companies, including those privatized from the public sector. Whereas TRIPs are restrictions that the WTO imposes, TRIMs (Trade-Related Investment Measures) are ones it aims to remove. Such measures constrain the freedom of foreign investors, and the Uruguay Round included a number of provisions prohibiting their use. The Doha Round aimed to go farther, by developing a wider investment agreement within the WTO framework. This had already been tried through the OECD, where negotiations on a Multilateral Agreement on Investment collapsed in 1998. The WTO attempt collapsed in Cancún in 2003. Many bilateral and regional agreements have been signed, however. They aim to secure the same treatment for foreign firms as for domestic ones, and to establish stronger rights for investors. The benefits to investing countries are clear. The impact on the recipients is more complicated.

As with the other components of the Doha agenda the effect on equilibrium economic welfare is small. The one-off global welfare gain has been estimated to be about $75 billion, or 0.25 per cent of GDP, with large uncertainty over what proportion goes to the investing countries and how much to the recipients (Nagarajan 1999). A much bigger benefit to developing countries could occur in the longer term if greater investor confidence led to greater foreign direct investment (FDI) and a sustained increase in economic growth.

Dirk Willem te Velde and Dirk Bezemer have found that investment provisions in regional trade agreements have led to a significant increase in FDI, particularly for the bigger countries of the regions (te Velde and Bezemer 2006). A review of other literature by Aaron Cosbey drew no solid conclusions (Cosbey 2005). When FDI does go up it will not necessarily lead to higher growth. The evidence reviewed by Cosbey shows no clear relationship. One of the reasons countries seek foreign investment is to improve their balance of payments, which allows a rise in imports (often of luxury goods) without having to increase exports. Governments that are eager to attract FDI often give incentives, and can get into bidding wars with each other that reduce any benefit to their own country while increasing the gains to transnational corporations (Hoekman and Saggi 2002). Investments in mergers and acquisitions add nothing to a country's capital stock, while transferring the profit on the capital from domestic to foreign investors.

The longer-term gains to developing countries occur when the technologies used by transnational corporations are taken up by local firms. Except in East Asia, successful technology transfer has been more the exception than the rule (UNDP 2003: ch. 12). Even here, the most successful of the countries relied only marginally on FDI for achieving it (Jomo 2005). As we saw in Chapter 4, the East Asian success was based on a wide range of trade-distorting measures that included incentives for domestic investment in targeted industries, limitations on foreign ownership, export requirements for foreign-owned companies and minimum levels of domestic content. Performance requirements of this nature are prohibited or severely restricted by the provisions of investment agreements.

The combination of technological investment and capital accumulation can be a powerful driver of socio-economic transformation and poverty reduction. If a country were able to negotiate an investment agreement that enhanced the development of its own technological capability and accelerated the accumulation of its own capital stock, it would almost certainly benefit. If it is persuaded to agree to one that puts the interests of foreign investors first and allows its developmental policy space to be restricted it will lose far more than anything its import-consuming elites might gain through a brief respite from their balance-of-payments constraints.

OVERALL IMPACT ON SUSTAINABLE DEVELOPMENT

Of the four Singapore issues only one, trade facilitation, is likely to make a positive contribution to sustainable development, and even there the effect is small. Bigger gains may be available from a country's own trade facilitation reforms, but the inclusion of such measures in a trade agreement provides no more than a useful mechanism for organizing cooperative action and international assistance.

The other three issues raised in Singapore were rejected by developing countries at Cancún, and rightly so. The provisions on government procurement would give a fairly small short-term economic benefit, at the cost of impairing or removing developing countries' freedom to employ simple and effective policy tools for economic management and long-term development. Those for competition have similar effects. There is a strong case for many developing countries to strengthen their own national competition policies, but they need to be tailored to each country's own particular economic and developmental needs and not bound by international rules. The proposals for investment favour investors, not the countries they invest in. They prohibit a wide range of measures that made a major contribution to the development successes of East Asia. The Singapore proposals on these three issues, and their equivalents in regional and bilateral agreements, all have a significant adverse impact on sustainable development.

9 | THE RULES OF THE GAME

The distribution of wealth, therefore, depends on the laws and
customs of society. The rules by which it is determined are what the
opinions and feelings of the ruling portion of the community make
them. (Mill 1909 [1848]: bk 2, ch. 1)

As well as applying constraints on trade barriers and the other measures
discussed in previous chapters, the WTO framework includes a number
of other rules without which the system could not function. The Doha
agenda aimed to revise many of these rules, while regional and bilateral
agreements often include variants or extensions of them.

In this chapter we examine the impacts of proposed changes to the
most significant of these rules. Most of the proposed changes have
mixed effects, beneficial in some countries and adverse in others, with a
net effect that is generally beneficial but small. Two items, the rules on
special and differential treatment and those for regional trade agreements,
remain serious cause for concern. In both cases the current rules have
major shortcomings that limit the development prospects of developing
countries, and the proposed changes do little or nothing to rectify this.

The chapter concludes with a discussion of one further item, trade
in oil and other mineral resources. This can have major adverse impacts
on sustainable development that are not addressed by the current
negotiation agenda.

WTO RULES

Compared with the United Nations, the World Trade Organization is
a tiny institution with a tiny budget. In some respects it achieves more,
through its highly effective system of global law. If a country fails to
comply with WTO rules it is not subject to the military force that the
UN struggles to muster, but pays a fine commensurate with the crime.
The use of trade sanctions is not the exclusive province of the WTO,
but for the WTO it is a routine matter. The aggrieved party files a case,
the defendant goes to court, and if found guilty must make amends or
suffer the consequences. Developed countries are accountable as well
as developing ones, and successful cases have been brought by some of
the poorest against some of the richest.

There are strong temptations to use the global legal powers of the WTO for issues other than the regulation of international trade. Much of the opposition to TRIPs and to three of the four Singapore issues (government procurement, competition and investment) is based on the argument that they are not trade issues and should not be regulated by the WTO. Conversely, the use of trade sanctions to address environmental concerns has led to the opposite argument, that the WTO should regulate such issues. This would make it easier to decide whether the use of sanctions should or should not be allowed when they breach WTO rules. Both of these extensions run the risk of sliding down a slippery slope. Unless the WTO were expanded to embrace all the expertise of all the relevant UN bodies, aiming to replace the UN, it is in no position to regulate anything other than trade.[15] Rogue states that refuse to comply with UN resolutions can be subjected to trade sanctions without foreign policy having to be conducted through the rules of the WTO. Even so, what the WTO does it does well.

Whether the WTO's rules are good or bad, it does not write them itself. It provides a forum in which the trade representatives of its member states write them. Nor does it pass judgement on whether they have been breached. That too is done by the trade representatives of member states, operating within the WTO framework. Most of the issues relate not to whether the WTO has too much or too little power, but to how member states use their own power.

The WTO framework is more than a meeting place in which members negotiate over what should be on a list of allowable tariff and non-tariff barriers. Its Dispute Settlement Mechanism is a vital component, along with rules that define the extent to which member states can give preferential treatment to some fellow members but not to others, and various other rules without which the system could not function effectively. The Doha agenda aimed to revise many of these rules, while regional and bilateral agreements often include variants or extensions of them.

Six groups of rules are particularly important, covering: dispute settlement; subsidies, countervailing measures and anti-dumping; technical and health standards; special and differential treatment; regional trade agreements; and trade and environment. Each of these is discussed separately below. As with other rules-based measures, economic models are incapable of modelling them with any confidence, and the assessment of impacts was based on other methods. A certain amount of quantitative information was available for some, while the assessment of others was based mainly on qualitative considerations and the findings of the research literature.

The SIA studies were confined to assessing the likely impacts of the rule changes, primarily for the WTO Doha agenda. For many of the issues we will go no farther. We will take a closer look at the rules on regional trade agreements, since they have a strong influence on the whole world trade regime. We will also consider some rules that have not been written but possibly should be.

DISPUTE SETTLEMENT

The WTO's Dispute Settlement Understanding (DSU) and Dispute Settlement Mechanism (DSM) were introduced with the creation of the WTO, and are widely regarded as a significant improvement on the system that operated under GATT (Delich 2002). Under the previous system rulings could only be adopted by consensus, with the result that they could be blocked by one of the parties to the dispute. Under the WTO system dispute settlement reports are adopted automatically unless there is a consensus to reject them. This makes it easier to make binding decisions, although appeals can still cause long delays in implementation while they work their way through the system. The Dispute Settlement Body that governs the DSM is composed of representatives of all WTO members. It appoints dispute resolution panels to handle each case. There is a permanent appellate body whose rulings are effectively final, although they can in principle be altered by full consensus of the Dispute Settlement Body. An advisory centre on WTO law has been established to provide advice and training, and to help make legal expertise more readily and cheaply available to developing countries. Developing countries still need to develop their own legal expertise, to avoid dependence on expensive experts from the developed ones (Raghavan 2000).

The WTO system has been used far more frequently than the less effective GATT system. Many of the cases have been brought by developing countries, against both developed countries and other developing ones. About half are settled at the consultation stage, and the rest have proceeded to a formal dispute. Relatively few have gone to appeal. Serious differences over compliance with rulings have arisen in only a handful of high-profile cases that have involved particularly sensitive national issues.

Despite these successes several difficulties are experienced (Hudec 2002; Delich 2002; UNEP/IISD 2005). The transparency in the system is limited, with no legal right for unsolicited submissions to be heard; a high level of expertise is needed to pursue a dispute and the costs are high; countries with sufficient market power to apply trade sanctions without damaging their own commercial interests are more readily able to press a case than smaller ones; and the provisions to address problems faced by developing countries have little operative content. The Doha agenda included negotiations on improvements and clarifications to address the issues.

The impact assessment study examined the likely impacts of changes that were considered to be realistic. These included clarification of procedures for unsolicited submissions (*amicus curiae* briefs), but with continued flexibility in accepting them. Other changes included greater transparency in making dispute submissions publicly available, and clarification of procedures in several other areas.

To estimate the likely influence of the changes the study examined the economic and other impacts of past disputes, some of which had been quantified. Those resulting from successful cases were highly significant, in opposite directions for the appellant and the defendant. No bias was identified between developed and developing countries. It was judged that the changes would have no more than a minor effect on equivalent impacts resulting from similar disputes in the future, or on future dispute rulings. The only significant impact identified was a small reduction in the time taken to reach an eventual settlement. This too would have economic impacts in opposite directions for the different parties, with a small but significant overall economic benefit. Social impacts would result directly from the economic ones through employment effects. Environmental effects would occur as a result of production changes, but were considered unlikely to be significant. The analysis fell well short of a comprehensive review of the dispute settlement system, but indicated that the Doha agenda for improving it was a positive one.

SUBSIDIES, COUNTERVAILING MEASURES AND ANTI-DUMPING

When a government subsidizes an industry it reduces the price of exports, which become more competitive against producers in other countries. The WTO rules do not ban subsidies, but restrict their use. If a government breaches the rules others can take action by imposing an import tax or other countervailing measure that would not otherwise be allowed. The Agreement on Subsidies and Countervailing Measures regulates both the use of subsidies and the measures that can be taken to counter them. Countries can also take similar action against dumping, in which a company sells a product in export markets at below its domestic price. The WTO does not regulate companies, only governments. The separate Anti-Dumping Agreement regulates the action that governments can take to counter dumping by other countries' companies.

After tariffs had been reduced in the Uruguay Round the use of countermeasures went up (Spinager 2002). This suggested that the countermeasures were increasingly being misused, to give the same level of protection as was previously obtained through tariffs. Meanwhile developing countries were calling for greater flexibility in using the measures they are designed to counter (Laird 2002). The Doha agenda aimed to reduce misuse by clarifying the rules, and also to strengthen the limitations on fisheries subsidies. These are a particular concern for environmental as well as economic reasons, since they can contribute to overfishing and the depletion of fish stocks. The same issue was picked up in the Doha agenda for Trade and Environment.

The impact assessment study for the fisheries sector indicated extremely mixed effects, which vary between developed and developing countries and between different countries in each group (Kleih et al. 2006). In general, countries with a significant fishing industry that is not heavily subsidized would benefit economically and socially from the removal of subsidies elsewhere, but with a likely increase in their own overfishing if the industry is not well regulated. Without effective regulation, free market competition in the industry tends to lead to overcapacity and depletion of stocks, with or without subsidies. In cases where subsidies have been used to help reduce overcapacity their removal might have the opposite effect on sustainability from that intended. Small-scale artisanal fishing tends to be more sustainable than large-scale commercial operations, and subsidies can play a similar role to agricultural ones in protecting small producers from import competition and helping to alleviate poverty. In these cases the social impacts could be significantly adverse with no benefit to the environment, and possible environmental losses from greater competition. In developing countries where fishing rights have been sold to foreign companies there may be a loss of income, but potential for positive social impacts for local fishers. In developed countries that have significant fishing subsidies the environmental impact of removing them would generally be beneficial, with a short-term adverse economic effect and a bigger beneficial one in the long term. In all countries strong regulation of the fishing industry is likely to be a key factor.

For other subsidies and countervailing measures and for anti-dumping, improving the WTO rules is expected to have a significant beneficial overall economic effect. Within this there would be an adverse effect, at least in the short term, for those cases and those countries which currently benefit from the trade distortion or the misuse of countermeasures. Among developed countries, the impact assessment indicated that the

USA would lose economically, while the EU would suffer a smaller loss. Among developing countries, the East Asian economies would gain. India and Argentina would lose. The development prospects of smaller and least developed countries that use subsidies to protect infant industries could be hampered by the changes. The environmental effects generally consist of a decline in environmental quality in some countries and an increase in others. They are not expected to be significant in developed countries, but in developing ones they may be somewhat larger, particularly for natural-resource-dependent industries such as forestry and fisheries.

TECHNICAL AND HEALTH STANDARDS

Countries generally aim to apply the same technical standards for manufactured products and standards of food safety to imports as they do to their domestic produce. The conditions under which they may do so are defined in the WTO Agreements on Technical Barriers to Trade (TBT) and Sanitary and Phytosanitary Measures (SPS). An area of concern for developing countries is the extent to which these measures constitute a barrier to their own exports, and their need for assistance with meeting international standards. One of the main concerns in developed countries is the extent to which the SPS agreement bars the application of animal welfare standards to imported products, which gives foreign suppliers a competitive advantage over domestic ones.

The WTO Doha agenda focused on technical and other assistance to developing countries for complying with the agreements and for improving their capacity to meet required standards for their products. The impact assessment indicated that the improvements achieved would be fairly minor, with a small economic benefit to both developing-country exporters and importing developed countries. Related social effects would be small, with no significant impact on the environment. The animal welfare issue has been addressed in EU submissions to the WTO, proposing that legal standards should be permissible, along with compensation for meeting the additional costs (European Commission 2003c). If this were agreed it would improve welfare standards for the exported products and benefit EU producers, at a cost to EU taxpayers. The economic impacts in the exporting countries would depend on the level of compensation and how it is allocated.

SPECIAL AND DIFFERENTIAL TREATMENT

The agreements made in the Uruguay Round included many pro-visions for special and differential treatment (SDT) for developing countries. These include longer transitional periods for implementing agreements, preferential treatment for tariffs and for liberalization of services, restraints on protective action taken against developing countries, greater freedom for them to provide agricultural subsidies, and provisions for technical assistance. Under certain conditions Article XVIII of GATT also allows a degree of freedom for supporting new industries.

During the preparations for the Seattle and Doha WTO conferences many developing countries expressed concerns over difficulties they faced in implementing their commitments in the Uruguay Round, the implementation of developed countries' commitments, and the interpretation of the SDT provisions and other WTO rules. The Doha conference agreed to consider the submissions that had been made and to review all special and differential treatment provisions, with the aim of strengthening them and making the commitments of developed countries more precise.

The impact assessment for the Doha negotiations drew the conclusion that satisfactory resolution of the implementation issues would have beneficial economic and social impacts in most developing countries, particularly the least developed, by reducing some of the potentially adverse impacts of the other aspects of the agenda. Many of the issues have yet to be resolved.

The limited effectiveness of SDT provisions in promoting the development of developing countries remains a major area of concern. Some of the concerns expressed by developing countries are less justified than others. As we saw in Chapter 5, greater access to developed-country markets for agricultural exports would tend to benefit large commercial producers rather than small farmers, with impacts on poverty that are more likely to be negative than positive. As we saw in Chapter 4, greater freedom to protect domestic manufacturing industries would not, on its own, accelerate industrial development. Those countries that have succeeded in developing have done so through carefully designed strategies implemented with considerable determination, which address rural development and urban development as an integrated whole. Even with the amendments that have been agreed and those that are still under discussion, the special and differential provisions in the WTO agreements are not sufficient to turn the Doha agenda into a development agenda.

Several suggestions have been made for modified approaches to SDT. We will return to them in Chapter 11 when we look at other possible reforms.

REGIONAL TRADE AGREEMENTS

Were it not for Article XXIV of GATT the European Union would be in flagrant breach of WTO rules. So would the North American Free Trade Agreement (NAFTA) between the USA, Canada and Mexico. Through an exemption to the WTO core principle of non-discrimination, the article permits the creation of a free trade area (FTA), in which a group of countries eliminates tariffs and other trade barriers between each other, or a customs union, in which they go farther to adopt common external tariffs for trade with other countries. Free trade areas and customs unions are collectively known as regional trade agreements (RTAs).

The core principles of the WTO require that every WTO member treat all other members equally. A free trade area is by definition discriminatory. Its members are exempted from the core principles of the WTO in order to permit the continued existence of the EU, NAFTA and other arrangements like them, and to allow other regional groups to form similar economic ties.

The European Union has gone beyond a free trade area and a customs union to become a single market, in which restrictions are also removed for the movement of capital and labour. There is much debate within some of its member states on whether these extra steps have gone too far, and even on whether staying in the free trade area is advisable. Similar debates occur in the NAFTA countries. Membership exposes each country to greater competition from the others, but at the same time allows their own export industries to tap the economies of scale of the regional market.

By discriminating in favour of fellow members preferential trade agreements are inherently trade-diverting. They increase trade with fellow signatories at the expense of trade with other countries. This results in an economic loss for the group as a whole and each country in it, as they import goods and services from each other that would be cheaper if bought elsewhere. The loss is at least partially countered by the gain from economies of scale. The trade diversion effect on other countries may also be countered if greater economic activity within the region leads to increased external trade. The economic impact on those countries, as well as within the region itself, depends on which effect is bigger.

Preferential agreements that reduce barriers for some goods and services but not for others tend to divert more trade than they create (Pomfret 2006). In order to retain a degree of non-discrimination the WTO exemption stipulates that any RTA must apply to substantially all trade between its parties. There is no clear definition of what is meant by substantial, or even what is meant by trade. The exemption also states that any interim arrangements during the creation of an RTA are permissible only if completed within a reasonable length of time. Other than in exceptional cases reasonable is taken to mean no more than ten years.

The lack of clarity stimulates some interesting debates. During one of the public meetings for one of the SIA studies the EC negotiator described how its offer of tariff reductions complied with WTO rules because it covered more than 95 per cent of all trade between the parties. The negotiator for the other side described how it covered only 35 per cent. The EC's calculation was based on the existing volume of trade. The alternative calculation was based on what the volume of trade would have been if all tariffs were removed.

Many developing countries have relatively few products with a comparative advantage in international markets. A high tariff on those few exportable products can reduce the trade in them to zero. The removal of tariffs on all other products will apply to substantially all of the minimal existing trade. It does not create a very substantial free trade area.

As well as falling a long way short of free trade, many regional trade agreements also fall a long way short of being regional. Europe is a recognizable region. So is North America. So are most of the groups of countries in other parts of the world that have attempted, often with little success, to achieve greater economic integration among themselves. The same cannot be said of Europe and China, nor of the USA and Morocco. Yet, within the loosely defined rules that attempt to enforce the WTO's core principle of non-discrimination, these and many other preferential trade agreements between distant parties are called regional trade agreements.

The bigger developing countries and newly industrialized ones are now joining in the game. In 1990 there were fewer than fifty such agreements. By the end of 2008 the number notified to the WTO was over four hundred and rising.

Some trade economists condemn these agreements out of hand.[16] Others see them as a second-best route to full multilateral liberalization through the WTO. Sheila Page makes a different case for some of them (Page 2007). She argues that in groups of countries with common historical, political and security ties the wider benefits may outweigh the economic costs, and can often be substantial. Where there are no such ties the agreements may be no more than an attempt by the stronger negotiating parties to get from the weaker ones what they have been stopped from getting through the WTO.

In groups of developing countries that are genuine regions doing their best to emulate Europe's Union these agreements have much to commend them. Some of the other preferential agreements might not do too much damage through tariff reductions, whose adverse effects might, in some cases, be outweighed by trade creation. It is possible that some of the agreements might also make some contribution towards multilateral liberalization through the WTO, but if so we have to ask why the WTO has retained non-discrimination as a core principle. They do nothing whatsoever to promote the WTO in their leverage of the Singapore issues and TRIPs-plus requirements, which were rejected in the WTO.

It was agreed at Doha that negotiations would take place on clarifying and improving these rules on RTAs, taking particular account of their developmental aspects. Little has been achieved beyond a requirement for the parties to release some of the details of what they have agreed.

TRADE AND ENVIRONMENT

The Doha agenda includes an item on trade and environment. Along with a few relatively minor issues it covers the liberalization of trade in environmental goods and environmental services, and the interactions between trade agreements and international environmental agreements.

The negotiations on manufactured goods cover all such goods, while those on liberalizing services cover all types of services. Environmental goods and services are singled out for special attention because their potential contribution to environmental protection may warrant greater liberalization than might otherwise be achieved. The liberalization of environmental services is a key objective for the EU and other developed countries. The liberalization of environmental goods is pursued by the countries that manufacture them. Developed countries make many of the goods used in the delivery of environmental services, while China in particular is a major supplier of products such as energy-efficient light bulbs and the photovoltaic cells used in solar electricity installations. Much of the negotiation has revolved around what goods should be classified as environmental goods. A pump used in a waste water treatment plant may be little or no different from one used in an oil refinery. In general, countries that have a comparative advantage in a particular product argue that it should be on the list.

As we saw in Chapter 6, the liberalization of environmental services can have environmental benefits, but not always. They are rarely as big as is claimed, and have often been accompanied by seriously adverse social effects. The issues are equally complex for environmental goods. In order to help meet its targets the EU subsidizes renewable energy, including solar energy installations. Despite its own trade barriers it imports many of the photovoltaic cells used to produce them. Much of the cost is the installation cost, so reducing the cost of the components may have little effect on the number of installations, or on the amount by which climate change is slowed. If the EU were to take advantage of the lower cost to reduce the subsidies, there would be no such effect and no environmental benefit. There would be a loss to EU suppliers of the components, a gain to foreign ones, corresponding gains and losses in employment, and an overall economic benefit to the EU from the cost saving. Meanwhile, the pollution created in the production of the goods would move from Europe to the countries that make them. The overall environmental impact of liberalization, in either direction, tends to be small.

Discussions and negotiations on the relationships between trade agreements and multilateral environmental agreements (MEAs) aim to make them more mutually supportive. As we saw in Chapter 7 for TRIPs and biodiversity, the issues arise because the provisions of many MEAs are imprecise. Some, such as the Convention on International Trade in Endangered Species and the Basel Convention on Control of Transboundary Movement of Hazardous Wastes, contain detailed provisions that restrict or prohibit trade with other countries in particular circumstances. The WTO has no mandate to define international environmental law and has to comply with these conventions. Other MEAs, such as the Convention on Biological Diversity, are less specific, and may do no more than define a broad goal. In these cases a trade agreement cannot be said to contravene international environmental law unless it represents a demonstrably major barrier to achieving that goal. Under GATT Article XX a trade restriction can be applied for environmental reasons, but only if it is demonstrably necessary, not arbitrarily discriminatory, and not a disguised restriction on international trade.

The discussions in the WTO are defined largely by case law, particularly by two high-profile cases brought against the USA (Mavroidis 2000; Jansen and Keck 2004), the tuna–dolphin dispute brought by Mexico and others, and the shrimp–turtle dispute brought by India, Pakistan and others. In both of these cases the USA had imposed import restrictions on goods produced using methods whose impacts on other species were considered to be more damaging than those of the methods used in the USA, and inadequate for achieving international goals. The WTO Appellate Body ruled that the restrictions were inadmissible on technical grounds, without resolving the question of whether either action consti-tuted a trade restriction disguised as environmental protection. In more recent cases US actions against EU regulations on genetically modified organisms and industrial chemicals have been cited as examples of WTO rules being used to challenge environmental protection measures (Risso and Wandel 2004). The actual disputes did not challenge the right to use measures to implement an MEA, but revolved around the way the measures were applied through the EU regulatory system.

The impact assessments drew the conclusion that the amendments under discussion in the Doha negotiations were likely to have some effect in reducing the likelihood of discriminatory actions being disguised as environmental measures, and in clarifying the circumstances when such measures can be used legitimately. They are unlikely to make a significant contribution to achieving the goals of MEAs. For that, the relevant multilateral environmental agreements themselves need to be far more specific in their requirements.

OVERALL IMPACT ON SUSTAINABLE DEVELOPMENT

None of the proposed rule changes is expected to have more than a minor effect on sustainable development. The economic effects are generally positive but insignificant, with small environmental or social benefits in some countries and the opposite effect in others. The rules on special and differential treatment (SDT) and regional trade agree-ments (RTAs), however, remain a serious cause for concern. The current rules in both areas have major shortcomings that limit the development prospects of developing countries. The changes being debated in the WTO do little or nothing to rectify this.

THE MISSING ELEMENT

Of all the many aspects of international trade that affect development and its environmental sustainability, the most influential by far is missing from the agenda. It may be covered to a degree in preferential trade agreements, but not in a way that promotes sustainable development, and not to any significant extent in the WTO. There are few barriers to be removed for trade in oil. There are few to be removed for trade in diamonds or most other valuable mineral resources. Countries that possess them have no difficulty in selling them. Those without them have little reason to erect barriers to buying them. Both parties gain in economic terms, at least in orthodox economic terms. This is despite the fact that selling oil, buying it and using it for its intended purpose is the biggest cause of climate change. For many resources the effects include massive local environmental despoliation. The social effects can be just as big. In the countries that possess the resource, and which might therefore seem to gain the most, the impacts are usually in the opposite direction to that expected by orthodox economic theory. The resource curse is off the agenda in trade negotiations.

Trade in precious natural resources is a classic example of David Ricardo's theory of comparative advantage, in this case also an absolute advantage, and of what it does to people. As Ricardo pointed out, when trade is free the consumers of the imported goods benefit from the lower prices, and entrepreneurs in all countries obtain a higher profit than if they invested in something else. Ricardo did not claim that anyone else would benefit. In the same book, his *Principles of Political Economy and Taxation*, he developed the theory first identified by Adam Smith and subsequently exploited by Marx, the labour theory of value. This describes how, unless a country's economy is continually diversifying and creating new demands for new skills, free market competition depresses wages to subsistence level. Neoclassical economic theory argues that the classical theory has been proved wrong by the high wages in high-income countries. The argument is invalid for two reasons. First, it ignores the fact that the economies of these countries are continually changing and continually creating demands for new skills. Second, it ignores the fact that they are at the core of an international trading system. The impacts of Ricardo's theory are felt not in the countries that import the resource, but in those that export it.

Statistical analyses of the relationship between a country's endowment of exportable natural resources and its success in increasing the incomes of the poor show an inverse correlation (Sachs and Warner 1995). The richer the country is in these resources, the poorer are its people. Of the countries that have escaped the curse the USA is the most obvious example, but for America it was easy. When it discovered black gold there was no market for it. It had to create one, through Henry Ford and the rest of American industry. For mineral-rich developing countries the market lies ready and waiting. Skilful entrepreneurs, military dictators, absolute monarchs and warring warlords can get very rich indeed without having to invest in the skills and earning power of the rest of the people. High-income countries that have discovered the resource after they have already industrialized have found it easier. Norway's policies are a model for others to follow.

Very few developing countries faced with the problem have succeeded in escaping it, and then only partly. Libya is one, though not without creating other problems, environmental as well as political. The country's economy is totally dependent on diminishing supplies of oil and natural gas, it imports half its food, and it is running out of water with which to grow the rest (Development Solutions 2009). Indonesia and Botswana have escaped to a degree, but few if any others (Auty 2000; Murshed 2002). Established development wisdom says the problem is bad governance. Of course it is. Free trade theorists rarely bother to ask why the governance is so bad. Under conditions of free trade the easy pickings of a high-value exportable natural resource corrupt a country's economy. A corrupt economy corrupts the people who run it.

The resource curse is not on the negotiating agenda for trade liberalization, and none of the sustainability impact assessments has addressed it in any depth. None of their recommendations has addressed it any more fully, leaving a gap that we will fill later. The studies have, however, made many recommendations for how all the other harmful effects of free trade might be countered. The task of acting on them with sufficient force to make a significant difference presents a considerable challenge.

THREE | **RESPONSES**

INTRODUCTION

The trade impact assessment studies have never been a purely
academic exercise. Their main purpose has always been to
identify ways in which the expected benefits of a trade agreement
might be enhanced and any adverse ones avoided or reduced to
an acceptable level. This might be through a change to the trade
agreement itself, or through parallel agreements or government
policies referred to as flanking measures.

In Chapter 10 we begin by examining the extent to which
the impact assessment studies have influenced EU trade policy,
either directly or indirectly. We then go on to examine the impact
of aid for trade, the main flanking measure used by the EU
and other donor countries as an adjunct to their trade policy.
Chapter 11 identifies the much stronger policy measures that
would be needed to make international trade more supportive of
globally sustainable development, and proposes corresponding
reforms to the WTO regime. The final chapter summarizes the
main impacts that have been identified in the book, reviews their
historical context, and concludes with a review of the evolving
global context in which reform of the world trade regime is
becoming increasingly important.

10 | OUTFLANKING MEASURES

And it ought to be remembered that there is nothing more difficult to take in hand, more perilous to conduct, or more uncertain in its success, than to take the lead in the introduction of a new order of things. Because the innovator has for enemies all those who have done well under the old conditions, and lukewarm defenders in those who may do well under the new. (Machiavelli 1515)

In this chapter we begin with a review of the extent to which the impact assessment studies have had any direct influence on EU trade policy. We then go on to examine their indirect influence, mainly through the efforts of parliamentarians and civil society groups. This too has been small. Finally we examine the highly questionable impact of Aid for Trade, the main flanking measure used by the EU and other donor countries to maximize the benefit they expect developing countries to get from trade liberalization and to counter any adverse effects.

A SELECTION OF ANSWERS

The first edition of Adam Smith's *Wealth of Nations* was published in 1776, the year after the outbreak of the American War of Independence. Smith devoted a large part of the book to promoting the American cause. He explained how England had prospered from its colonies in the New World, and how it would prosper even more if it were to abandon its constraints on their development. Americans took heart from Smith's advice. The government of King George III ignored it. America had to fight the war for another seven years, and win it, before it could demonstrate that Smith's prediction was correct.

None of the reports that have been published in Europe's trade impact assessment programme can compare with Adam Smith in their analytical prowess, their eloquence or their boldness. None has been brave enough to tell the king that his policy was just plain wrong. Most, more tactfully, have assessed it as the curate would his egg, good in parts. All have recommended changes, some quite radical. The response has been limited.

The European Commission undertook to publish positioning papers giving official responses to the findings of each of the studies. These have

to go through the policy-making process itself, which entails consultation with member states and approval by the committee in which their
representatives jointly define European trade policy under Article 133 of
the Treaty of Amsterdam (the '133 Committee'). This takes time. Only
two official responses have been published within a year, and most of
those issued so far have taken nearly two years. Several have yet to be
released, long after the negotiations have finished.[17] In those positioning
papers that have been produced the individual responses tend to fall
into one of five main categories: the Commission disagrees with the
findings; sufficient action is already being taken; possible new action is
under consideration; more detailed analysis is needed before decisions
on action can be taken; new action is proposed. Where the response
is in the last group, the proposed action has tended not to be specific,
such as raising awareness or reinforcing an existing policy.

There has been no positioning paper for the final overall assessment
of the WTO Doha agenda, nor for several of its more detailed studies,
nor the assessment of the EU–Chile trade agreement, nor the impact
study of the Euro-Mediterranean Free Trade Area. The final report of
the Mediterranean study presented thirty-seven specific recommendations. Three of its six overall conclusions called for major policy changes
in both the EU and its Mediterranean partners (IARC 2007b). No
official response has yet been published. For the EU's partnership
agreements with the African, Caribbean and Pacific (ACP) countries
the impact assessment reports presented a total of 207 detailed recommendations, many of which called for significant changes to EU policy
(PricewaterhouseCoopers 2005, 2006). After the last of these reports
was issued an additional specific agreement was approved under the
framework contract between the EC and the company responsible for
the study, which was then engaged to prepare a summary report on
the project (PricewaterhouseCoopers 2007). The EC issued its official
response within eight months of this being published. With one caveat
for what it termed transition arrangements for sugar, the positioning
paper described how the EC's existing policy already implemented all
twelve of the recommendations presented in the summary report. There
has been no official response to the more innovative 207.

Impact assessment as introduced in the US National Environmental
Policy Act aimed to contribute to a process of rational and publicly
accountable decision-making in which development decisions are transparent and based on a sound knowledge of the likely impacts. NEPA
got reasonably close to this, as have the EU's EIA Directive and many
of the other environmental impact assessment systems that NEPA

spawned throughout the world. Most of the assessments carried out under these laws are for proposals made by private sector developers, seeking approval from government authorities. In such cases the authority's objectives are, in principle if not always in practice, independent of those of the proponent. When the proponent of a policy is itself the competent authority the process is not so straightforward.

INDIRECT INFLUENCES

Political science analysis of impact assessment systems indicates that different systems are introduced for different reasons, some of which may not be immediately apparent (Radaelli 2005). Much of the analysis suggests that some have goals that are more closely related to how objectives are achieved than to defining what they are. When political issues are disguised as technical ones the policy-making process can become less accountable rather than more. Decisions may still be rational, but their objectives may not be the same as those that are publicly announced. As we saw in Chapter 2, the role of impact assessment is particularly problematic when it is applied to trade policy. No one government can define a trade agreement, nor even announce its own policy except in the broadest of terms. The specific aims of its negotiating mandate have to remain confidential in order to avoid revealing its hand to the countries it is negotiating with. Europe's negotiators negotiate for Europe, not for the countries that experience the most significant of the adverse impacts. Negotiators for most of those countries have less economic bargaining power. They often negotiate on behalf of interest groups whose concerns for social, environmental or developmental impacts may not be very high. In such circumstances the sustainability impact assessments introduced by Pascal Lamy will have done well to have any influence at all, other than in giving civil society groups the opportunity to air their views less disruptively than they otherwise might.

When we did our own assessment of the impact of the impact assessments we did identify some influence. Although our examination of the EC's positioning papers revealed little evidence of a significant policy response, we did see some evidence that negotiations had been influenced in some cases, whether or not that had been due to the position adopted by EC negotiators. For the Mediterranean study there was a close parallel between recommendations made in the first of the impact assessment reports and the published actions agreed at the ministerial summit for which the report had been timed. This followed strong representations based on the impact assessment findings from parliamentarians and civil society groups. For the ACP study and several others civil society groups made extensive use of the findings in their representations to governments. For the ACP study negotiators from both sides were actively involved in the impact assessment process, and many of the views expressed by ACP representatives reflected the study findings.

We used a questionnaire survey to solicit stakeholder perceptions of whether policy had changed as a result of the studies, with responses from NGOs, the private sector, EC trade negotiators and other EC officials (George and Kirkpatrick 2009). Of these 59 per cent considered that the overall impact was low or very low, with no statistically significant difference between the different types of stakeholder. Over 80 per cent of respondents thought that the influence on trade agreements or non-EU domestic policy was low or very low, although they perceived a somewhat greater influence on EU domestic policy and development aid programmes.

Beyond this we observed what we judged to be a significant improvement in coordination within the European Commission, combined with the provision of information that strengthened the hand of non-trade officials. During steering committee meetings with EC officials on the SIA studies we often found ourselves on the sidelines as interested observers while lively debates took place between representatives of different EC departments, for example on EU biofuels policy and its interactions with trade policy. These suggested that even livelier discussions may have been going on behind closed doors for which the study findings were serving a useful purpose. For some of the studies we observed a similar effect through the active engagement of parliamentarians, both in Europe and in some of its trading partners. The Mediterranean study triggered a resolution in the Euro-Mediterranean Parliamentary Assembly and a question in the European Parliament to which the Trade Commissioner was required to respond (EMPA 2006; European Parliament 2006). He went no farther than to say that the findings would be taken into account.

The recommendations made in impact assessment reports identify how the beneficial impacts of the proposed trade agreement might be enhanced, and how the adverse ones might be avoided or reduced to an acceptable level. Relatively few of these are for changes to the trade agreement itself. Most, known as parallel measures or flanking measures, apply to other aspects of government policy that might be changed in order to complement or counter the effects of trade policy. They include measures within a broader cooperation agreement between the trading partners, and others that may be implemented independently by individual governments. What little evidence we found that policy had changed as a result of the studies generally related to these flanking measures, and not to the trade agreements themselves.

Some of the most important flanking measures are those related to global impacts. Several of the studies have recommended that these should be countered by strengthening global regulation, knowing full well how difficult it is. None has been bold enough to advise the European Commission to halt all further efforts to liberalize trade until fully effective global agreements are in place to halt climate change and biodiversity loss. The Commission can justifiably argue that it is already trying to do what the recommendations say it should. The same applies to efforts to strengthen social and environmental regulation within developing countries. To the extent that assistance from developed ones can help, it is already being given. Some of the studies have recommended a tougher approach for local impacts, if not for global ones. They have proposed that some of the measures in the trade agreement should not be implemented without an effective mechanism for monitoring relevant social and environmental conditions, whose results demonstrate sufficient improvement to accommodate the adverse effects of the agreement. No such approach has yet been introduced.

Many of the most commonly proposed flanking measures are in the form of trade-related development assistance, aiming to help developing countries take action to maximize the benefits of a trade agreement and counter any adverse effects. Whether or not the EU has felt the need to adjust its aid programmes to allow for the findings of the studies, it does, along with other donor countries and international institutions, provide considerable trade-related assistance.

AID FOR TRADE

When the Uruguay Round was concluded in 1994 it was recognized that the least developed countries would need assistance with implementing some of its provisions, particularly for product standards and TRIPs. In 1997 the WTO joined forces with the World Bank, the IMF, UNCTAD, UNDP and the International Trade Centre (ITC) to develop an Integrated Framework for Trade Related Technical Assistance, aiming to make trade a mainstream component of development initiatives. The Hong Kong ministerial meeting of the WTO endorsed the integrated framework and adopted aid for trade as a key component of its agenda.

The Aid for Trade Task Force set up by Pascal Lamy when he became director general of the WTO identified two main areas of support, covering both previous trade-related assistance and a wider agenda. The previous assistance covered activities such as training trade officials, implementing trade agreements, complying with rules and standards or promoting investment. The wider aid for trade agenda includes building ports and other infrastructure, increasing productive capacity, financial assistance with the loss of tariff revenues or the erosion of preferences, and assistance with meeting other trade-related needs (WTO 2006).

The aim of aid for trade, as defined at the Hong Kong meeting, is to help developing countries build the supply-side capacity and trade-related infrastructure they need to implement and benefit from WTO agreements, and more broadly to expand their trade. The EU strategy on aid for trade states it slightly differently, as being to help developing countries integrate more fully into the rules-based world trading system, and to more effectively use trade in promoting the eradication of poverty in the context of sustainable development (Council of the European Union 2007).

The EU strategy aims to ensure that increases in aid for trade are not achieved at the expense of other priorities considered to be essential for reaching the Millennium Development Goals. This does not mean that non-priority development assistance would not be cut, either in the EU or by other donors that give aid for trade. If trade liberalization genuinely is the most effective means of reducing poverty, the diversion of the available funds into aid for trade could be highly beneficial. At least some of the funding, however, is needed not to enhance the potential benefits of a trade agreement, but to counter its adverse effects. As Robin Koshy points out, the adjustment costs are borne up front, whereas the potential rewards could take decades (Koshy 2006). Countries that lose their preferences lose them as soon as other countries' tariffs are cut. Other economic sectors are likely to take many years to respond. In countries where tariffs are cut, government revenue falls as soon as they are cut, and needs to be replaced straight away. In import-dependent developing countries any reduction in European or American agricultural subsidies increases the cost of food for the whole country, particularly the urban poor. The reforms may be essential for those countries' own agricultural development, but this takes time.

Analysis of past trade-related assistance indicates that its allocation to different countries may not have been driven by their needs (Calì 2007). The biggest adjustment costs are experienced by the least developed countries, which also face the biggest difficulties in reaping the potential benefits. Between 2001 and 2004 they received only 21 per cent of total aid for trade. Even when a country can secure a firm commitment for the level of assistance it will receive, there is absolutely no guarantee that money spent on technical assistance will deliver what is expected. Michael Finger called aid for trade under the WTO Doha agenda a bonanza for consultants which would do nothing for development (Finger 2006).

As we saw in Chapter 5, the dramatic reductions in poverty that have been achieved in South-East Asia and now China have come from releasing the potential of small farmers, not from large commercial exporters. The aid for trade agenda has little to say about small-scale farms. It has a lot to say about increasing the productivity of large exporting ones, and, by inference, their incentives to take productive land from the small ones. It has little or nothing to say about assistance for the non-commercial agricultural research and extension schemes that played such an important role in South-East Asia and China.

Aid for trade is specifically intended to help developing countries increase their productivity, and hence reduce their prices, for those things that high-income countries want to buy. It does little or nothing to help them produce those high-earning things that high-income countries would sooner produce themselves. It has in the past, particularly in the form of trade preferences, helped some of the poorer developing countries develop their manufacturing capability for low-wage exporting industries such as footwear and clothing. It has done almost nothing to help them acquire the technological capabilities that would allow them to increase their skill levels, upgrade their productivity and remain competitive when those preferences are lost (UNCTAD 2007). It is aid for trade, not aid for development. It assumes that the two are the same.

Dirk Willem te Velde and others at the Overseas Development Institute have identified a conflict of interest between the provision of at least some forms of aid for trade and the negotiation of a trade agreement (te Velde et al. 2006). The interests of the countries that provide the aid may diverge from or even oppose those of the countries they are negotiating with. They suggest that an honest broker is needed.

The EU strategy on aid for trade goes beyond the objectives defined by the WTO task force to provide assistance with implementing trade-related rules and regulations for competition policy and law, investment, transparency in public procurement and the extension of intellectual property rights beyond those agreed in TRIPs. This is the EU's trade agenda, not the WTO's. It is being pursued by America as well as Europe, having been rejected by the WTO membership. They believe that it will assist the development of developing countries while promoting their own. The countries that blocked the proposals in the WTO do not believe it. Nor, we might suspect, would an honest broker.

The UN Conference on Trade and Development has identified four changes that are needed to make aid more supportive of development, all of which are highly relevant to making aid for trade more supportive of trade for development (UNCTAD 2007). At the top of the list is a rapid increase in assistance for agricultural research and development for the least developed countries. Second, non-agricultural technological learning and innovation should be prioritized, including the use of donor-supported physical infrastructure projects to positively promote the development of domestic design and engineering capabilities, along with support for enterprise-based technological learning. Third, technological development issues should be included in the diagnostic analysis for selecting aid interventions. Fourth, trade preferences and assistance should explicitly facilitate the diffusion of best practices to domestic firms within a country and encourage technological upgrading.

From the above discussion we might add several others, and one in particular. Some kind of honest broker might be needed to ensure that no new measures are added to the agenda which promote the interests of the donor above those of the recipient.

The current trade liberalization agenda may not be as bad as the colonial agenda of King George III, but it is a bad agenda. Aid which reinforces that agenda is bad aid. It will counter few of the adverse impacts of liberalization, will do little to ensure that the potential benefits are experienced by the countries that most need them, and will do nothing to make global development sustainable development. Donors should think less about their own short-term interests and more about the global interest, in the short term, the medium term and the long term. International trade is too important for the world as a whole to be governed under the rules that are currently proposed, or even as they currently are. They are based on the same economic principles as led to the current global economic crisis. The time is ripe for reform.

11 | REWRITING THE RULES

The wise and virtuous man is at all times willing that his own private interest should be sacrificed to the public interest of his own particular order or society. He is at all times willing, too, that the interest of this order or society should be sacrificed to the greater interest of the state or sovereignty, of which it is only a subordinate part. He should, therefore, be equally willing that all those inferior interests should be sacrificed to the greater interest of the universe, to the interest of that great society of all sensible and intelligent beings. (Smith 1982 [1759]: 245)

In previous chapters we have seen how the current trade liberalization agenda does little to help achieve globally sustainable development, and aims to reinforce a regime that has the opposite effect. In this chapter we make use of these findings to identify the reforms that would be needed to make a positive contribution to the development of developing countries instead of hindering it, to reduce world poverty rather than increasing it, and to help stem climate change, biodiversity loss and all the other effects through which economic development has become environmentally unsustainable.

We begin by examining the fears of protectionism that have been associated with any move to restrict international trade, particularly in relation to the current global economic crisis. We see how the crisis presents an opportunity for change, but note the limited extent to which any currently viable form of global governance can promote the global interest above competing national interests. We examine the role played by Bretton Woods in rebuilding the world economy after the crisis of the 1930s, and identify the need for a new international conference of similar stature which combines the economic and environmental issues. We then explore the reforms to the world trade regime which such a conference might enable. We begin with a proposal to abolish the single undertaking, through which the rules covering different aspects of trade are bargained against each other. We go on to examine the necessary reforms for each of these aspects, covering manufactured goods, agriculture, services, the Singapore issues and intellectual property rights. The chapter ends with a discussion of other global issues that would have to be addressed in parallel, to help steer the world out of crisis and into a new era.

THE GLOBAL INTEREST AND THE NATIONAL INTEREST

Eight months after the 1929 Wall Street crash America raised its barriers to imports through the Smoot-Hawley Tariff Act of 1930. Other countries followed suit, as had been feared by over a thousand economists who had petitioned against it. In urging governments not to take similar action in response to the 2008 crash *The Economist* has asserted that the 1930 act 'turned a stockmarket collapse into a crippling, decade-long Depression' (Economist 2008a). It declares that 'everybody sensible scoffs at Reed Smoot and Willis Hawley', the senator from Utah and the congressman from Oregon responsible for this feat (Economist 2009a). It quotes a chorus of condemnation describing their act as poison, madness, asinine (Economist 2008b). When faced with a challenge to their fundamental beliefs, economists can become quite passionate.

Some of this alarm should be taken seriously. If protectionism were to degenerate into the rampant nationalism that infused Germany and Japan in the 1930s the whole world would be in for a torrid time. The chance of that happening is made higher, not lower, by impassioned promotion of unsound economic theories.

The Economist is not always so passionate. It has presented the more reasoned views of other economists without scoffing at them or choosing to exclude them from 'everybody sensible'. Few economists, it reports, think the Smoot-Hawley tariff was one of the principal causes of the Depression (ibid.). America had already imposed bigger tariff rises in 1922, mainly in an attempt to solve the economic and social problems caused by massive American overproduction, especially in agriculture. The industry had expanded rapidly during the First World War in response to declining production in Europe, followed by falling American exports when Europe recovered. When the attempt to solve the problem failed, Herbert Hoover promised yet more tariff rises in his 1928 election campaign, and delivered them through the efforts of Smoot and Hawley. Had they paid more attention to the environmental consequences of overproduction they might have done the opposite, at least for agriculture. They would not have prevented the Depression, but they might have made its pain a little less severe by heading off the looming dust bowl of Steinbeck's *Grapes of Wrath*.

The Smoot-Hawley Tariff Act was bad for America, at least in terms of magnifying the consequences of unsustainable agriculture, but had little effect on a global depression that was already under way. World trade had already begun its downward spiral for entirely different reasons, as has happened again now. The decline in trade that goes with a shrinking world economy has been seized as yet another pretext for liberalizing measures with their own distinct purposes, some of which serve the long-term global interest while others have narrower and darker motives.

The current global crisis presents an opportunity for change. Economic structures and trade structures are undergoing a radical and painful transformation, as the multi-trillion-dollar financial losses are reallocated and absorbed within each country's real economy of people and productive physical capital. In parallel the credibility of the neoliberal orthodoxy has crumbled, opening the way for policies whose foundations are sounder.

In seizing the opportunity to change the rules of trade in favour of environmentally sustainable global development we need to bear in mind that the world is not a democracy. As Adam Smith observed in his *Theory of Moral Sentiments*, the 'wise and virtuous' should, in theory, be prepared to sacrifice the interest of their country for the sake of the whole world as willingly as they sacrifice their personal interest for the sake of their country. In practice, continued Smith, 'the care of the universal happiness of all rational and sensible beings is the business of God and not of man'. Man was allotted a much humbler department, 'the care of his own happiness, of that of his family, his friends, his country', in that order and no more. The humble human being, Smith advised, should avoid the charge levelled against Mark Antony, that while he 'contemplated the prosperity of the universe, he neglected that of the Roman Empire' (Smith 1982 [1759]: 246).

No such charge can be levelled against Smith. Despite the great moral philosopher's personal empathy with the whole human race, his second book, *An Inquiry into the Nature and Causes of the Wealth of Nations*, was first and foremost an inquiry into how the wealth of the emergent British Empire had been created and how it could be maintained.

Since then new technologies of human communication have increased our awareness of the global society around us, along with the extent to which any and all of us care about the well-being of its more distant members. Our awareness of its fragility has also risen, through greater understanding of the biological and physical science of the planet we all share. There is more scope than before for enforceable rules that put the interests of global society above those of dominant empires or the richest and most powerful nations, but it is still sorely limited. Any realistic proposal for rewriting the rules of international trade must take that into account.

A NEW KIND OF AGREEMENT

After the 1929 crash the world economy was eventually put back on its feet through the international agreements forged at Bretton Woods in 1944. There is now much talk of another conference to perform the same task, a second Bretton Woods. The various summits so far have fallen well short of that. What is needed is a genuine equivalent of Bretton Woods and more.

Little can be achieved by a conference that is rushed into place in the hope of fixing an economic crisis whose fundamental causes are beyond the comprehension of its delegates. Bretton Woods was attended not by the leaders whose failed policies had caused the crisis but by those who had replaced them, advised by a new set of advisers. The USA is now relatively well placed in that respect but other influential countries have yet to catch up. Even then their leaders will find it hard to come to terms with the realities of the current state of the world. The deliberations at Bretton Woods were influenced not just by financial collapse but by ten years of depression, the horrors of fascism and five more years of world war. By then it was abundantly clear that, despite the rebuttal of the challenges from Germany and Japan, the British Empire was no longer the dominant force in the world. Bretton Woods would not have been possible without the years of hard bargaining that preceded it, between Britain and the number-one rising global power, the USA. Their Atlantic Charter provided the foundation for the wider international agreement of Bretton Woods. The success of any new conference is likely to depend on a similar prior process of building unanimity between established power and rising power. If America can achieve that it will have demonstrated its qualities of world leadership even more impressively than it did at Bretton Woods.

Even that will not be enough. The Bretton Woods conference succeeded because it was not confined to economic management. Its recipe for recovery included creating the International Bank for Reconstruction and Development, now the World Bank, specifically charged with rebuilding war-torn countries and helping developing ones develop. The same need is no less urgent now. It requires a radical reappraisal of the World Bank's mandate and of whether it is even the right approach.

Yet more is needed. The leaders of all the countries represented at the 1992 Earth Summit in Rio de Janeiro accepted that economic management, environmental management and social development are all intricately interconnected, such that none of the problems could be solved without addressing them together as an integrated whole. Neoliberalism elbowed Rio to one side, taking the view that its own economic approach was all that was needed because it integrated everything. The Stern report on the economics of climate change showed how wrong that was. It called climate change the greatest market failure the world has ever seen (Stern 2006). The economic crisis and the climate crisis have to be addressed together if a solution is to be found to either. It is not just a new Bretton Woods which is needed, but a newly combined Bretton Rio.

The twin economic and climate crises cannot be fixed by economists alone, particularly those whose neoclassical theory has proved so limited in its applicability to the economic behaviour it attempts to describe. They will have to get together with other economists, heterodox as well as orthodox, political as well as mathematical, along with the members of the IPCC and globally respected experts in every discipline of development and environment for as long as it takes to reach a reasonable degree of consensus on their advice to presidents and prime ministers. Their conference would then be in a position to restore economic management to the place it had at Bretton Woods, subordinate to the wider goals of human development and not their defining principle.

A global conference endowed with that level of authority and that quality of advice holds every prospect of steering the world out of crisis and into a new era. Among its powers it would have full licence to abolish the WTO, replace it with some other institution, hand its powers to other global bodies, revise its mandate or totally rewrite it. In the light of the impacts identified in the SIA studies the regulatory role that is currently performed by the WTO should not be abolished. It should be strengthened, not weakened, but not with the mandate the WTO currently has.

THE SINGLE UNDERTAKING

The WTO inherited its *raison d'être* from GATT, the General Agreement on Tariffs and Trade, which became the third member of the global triumvirate established through Bretton Woods. Along with the World Bank and the IMF, GATT and then the WTO became increasingly enlisted to the neoliberal cause from the 1980s on, but in itself GATT still serves its original straightforward purpose, to regulate trade in manufactured goods.

It was originally planned that GATT would cover all types of goods, but attempts to liberalize agriculture did not begin in earnest until the

Uruguay Round's Agreement on Agriculture of 1994. The General Agreement on Trade in Services (GATS) was added at the same time, along with the creation of the WTO to supervise all three. This enabled the introduction of the single undertaking, through which concessions on any one of these agreements could be traded for concessions on another, or threats of sanctions under one could be used as leverage to get agreement on another.

By then neoliberalism had taken hold. Its overarching goal of free trade in everything gave the single undertaking a certain rationale, but that has now gone. It no longer makes any sense to treat freer trade in services as the equivalent of freer trade in agricultural produce and bargain one against the other. As has been identified throughout the book, many of the biggest adverse impacts of the current trade liberalization agenda are a direct result of the single undertaking. It should be scrapped.

Unless the WTO were dissolved it would continue to supervise the cross-cutting rules that apply to all aspects of international trade. This includes the WTO rules on regional trade agreements, which should be considerably strengthened. They were introduced to permit the existence of the European Union, the North American Free Trade Agreement and similar regional groups. They should be confined to that purpose only. In all other cases the WTO core principle of non-discrimination should apply in full, such that all non-regional preferential agreements involving a WTO member state are banned. As well as being responsible for these cross-cutting rules the WTO could also continue supervising the specific agreements covering each type of trade, but separately, not making one dependent on another.

The all-or-nothing approach adopted with the creation of the WTO was originally used by rich countries as a means of exercising power over poor ones. The tables have, in part, been turned. China, India, Brazil and several smaller developing countries now have sufficient economic bargaining power to exploit the single undertaking for their own ends, trading concessions in one area for commercial advantage gained in another. Having been created as an instrument of neoliberal power, the WTO has been turned into a global cattle market. For the benefit of the world as a whole the new balance of power within the WTO, or above it if necessary at a conference of world leaders, should give priority to dismantling the single undertaking. This would allow manufacturing trade, agricultural trade and services trade to be managed according to their own specific needs.

TRADE IN MANUFACTURED GOODS

As we saw in earlier chapters the impacts of fully liberalizing trade in manufactured goods include good ones as well as bad ones. The good ones reinforce what GATT already achieves. It reduces the scope for industrialized countries and newly industrializing ones to wage trade wars with each other, and enables them to produce goods more cheaply through the economies of scale of global markets. The bad ones are felt mainly by those developing countries that have barely even started industrializing, plus adjustment effects as people everywhere lose their jobs and have to find a new one, plus a range of environmental effects that are felt in particular places or throughout the world.

To maximize the benefits of GATT the industrialized countries need to fully implement it. They have already reduced their bound tariff rates to low levels on average, particularly for the semi-processed goods they want to import. For the higher-added-value products in which each country specializes they have kept them high. To get the most out of GATT they need to completely eliminate tariffs and non-tariff barriers for these products as well, and ban the subsidies that have become their protectionist measure of choice.

There will be people who lose their jobs as a consequence, some of whom may never get another. This would be on top of the same but bigger effects from the global economic crisis. It should not be done lightly. Nor can it be. The industrialized countries are sufficiently democratic to hold governments back from reducing trade barriers any faster than can be accommodated tolerably smoothly, and to press them into adopting domestic policies on education, training and social support to help people through. The long-term benefits would be considerable. The economies of scale are a minor factor. The completion of GATT would lock into place a globally interconnected manufacturing economy in which firms compete with each other but countries do not. Without that, a decade that resembles the 1930s could easily degenerate into one that resembles the 1940s.

The newly industrialized countries are already part of this process and would join the established ones in negotiating the full implementation of GATT. Other developing countries are currently covered by a range of provisions for special and differential treatment that are nowhere near sufficient to avoid the adverse impacts that we have identified. Many suggestions have been made for how SDT might be made more effective (Stevens 2002; Hoekman et al. 2004; Keck and Low 2004; Kleen and Page 2005). Most of these depend on clearer definitions of one or more categories of developing country, and criteria by which they would graduate through various levels of qualification for special treatment. Joseph Stiglitz and Andrew Charlton have proposed a much simpler approach, in which all countries, developed or developing, give free market access to all developing countries whose GDP and GDP per capita are smaller than their own (Stiglitz and Charlton 2005). As well as using criteria that are easy to apply, this has several other advantages, but provides little protection for the countries that most need it. Once the most favoured nation (MFN) tariffs that industrialized countries apply to each other have fallen to zero, poorer countries would get no special or differential treatment at all.

Most of these proposals for strengthening SDT assume that the single undertaking will remain in place, so that the provisions would apply to agricultural as well as manufactured goods. Once the two are separated an even simpler approach becomes possible. GATT would revert to its original role as an association of countries that consider themselves sufficiently highly industrialized to need to belong. Those that choose not to join would be free to raise their tariffs as high as they like, and protect their infant industries as much as they like. There may be no need for GATT to define what tariffs members should apply to non-members. If the EU were to apply import barriers to products from a highly impoverished developing country that it does not apply to the USA, and at the same time claim that it is helping that country develop, a significant number of European voters would complain vociferously. As long as the industrial exports of such countries remain small, the industrialized countries have nothing to lose from taking the easy option of applying MFN tariffs universally, even when they have fallen to zero. It is only when a country's infant industries have become sufficiently established to begin to pose a threat that any GATT member should feel the need to impose differential tariffs or quotas. At that point the country concerned would need to consider whether it has become sufficiently industrialized to join GATT. There might be some advantage from defining different categories of membership for different types of product, but this would lose the benefit of simplicity.

The industrialized countries are unlikely to welcome such an approach. Their ability to export high-added-value goods and import low-added-value ones in return would be curtailed. Achieving it would be heavily dependent on a high-level global agreement, promoted in particular by the bigger and more powerful developing countries, based on a recognition that development and poverty reduction really do matter, not just for the sake of altruism, but for the future economic and political stability of the world.

A global agreement of this nature would not need to address all the adverse environmental impacts of manufacturing liberalization. Many are specific to individual countries and are under their own control. Countries whose industrial exports are set to rise need to weigh the economic gains against their own environmental costs, and strengthen their regulatory regimes fast enough to keep pace with expanding production. It is only the global costs which need a global agreement, particularly for climate change. Emissions from transport would increase. So would carbon leakage, through which high-income countries offload a large proportion of the emissions arising from their consumption to the countries that produce the goods (Tao Wang and Watson 2009). This is already a key issue in climate negotiations, and needs to be carried through into a wider agreement that combines the environmental and economic issues.

AGRICULTURAL TRADE

Only a limited number of countries are significant producers of manufactured goods, but all are significant agricultural producers. Binding rules on agricultural trade should therefore continue to apply to all WTO members, but not as currently defined.

Most of the adverse impacts that we have identified result from the attempt to liberalize agriculture through the 1994 Agreement on Agriculture and its reinforcement at Doha. This applies to the removal of import tariffs and domestic subsidies in Europe, America and Japan as well as in developing countries. They have been heavily criticized on the grounds that they limit developing countries' exports, but the analysis presented here does not support that case.

The main beneficiaries would be the big commercial operators, not small farmers, nor, in many cases, the workers on exporting farms. In some parts of the world they are employed as slave labour. Employing more of them would not benefit them. Nor would it benefit the subsistence farmers whose land is taken by large ones in order to increase their exports at the lowest possible labour cost. To avoid the adverse impacts the attempt to liberalize agriculture should be abandoned and reversed, except for key provisions that contribute positively to food security, poverty reduction and the long-term development of developing countries.

The most important liberalization measure that needs to be retained and strengthened is the removal of export subsidies by all countries. Those provided by high-income countries benefit the urban poor in many developing countries, but at the cost of the livelihoods of those countries' own farmers, their ability to supply their own food and their longer-term ability to develop. To avoid major adjustment impacts the subsidies need to be phased out gradually, but with a clear deadline for when they will have been eliminated.

By contrast domestic support should not be eliminated, or even discouraged, whether in Europe, America or anywhere else. It serves an entirely different purpose, to ensure that a country can feed its own people. It can have the same effect as export subsidies in reducing world market prices and damaging other countries' agriculture, but that can be dealt with through an additional provision in the agreement. Any subsidy would have to be accompanied by a corresponding export tax. In situations where food aid is needed it should be provided for that purpose only, on a strictly temporary basis, and not converted into food dependency through WTO rules.

As well as its perverse effects on the world's ability to feed itself, agricultural liberalization is among the biggest drivers of climate change and declining global biological diversity. Freer trade in biofuels can make a positive contribution in some specific circumstances, but the necessary international controls have yet to be developed, applied and demonstrated to be effective. The radical reforms that are needed would have to be through a comprehensive global agreement covering the economic, social and environmental issues. All the reforms to the Agreement on Agriculture would have to be phased in over several years to minimize disruption of world markets, but even then there would be major opposition from many commercial interests in many countries, both rich and poor.

Many developing countries export little other than agricultural produce, so constraining their opportunities to export would limit their ability to import. The effect would be felt by the higher-income groups that consume the imports, not by the poor. Less freedom to export agricultural produce would not hamper these countries' ability to develop. It would increase their incentives to do so. The trade reforms would reinforce the influence of the UNCTAD proposals discussed in the previous chapter, for steering development assistance away from low-wage exports, towards increasing people's incomes through technological learning and innovation.

The reforms are unlikely to be welcomed by low-income country elites, who depend on agricultural exports to pay for their imported luxuries and other consumer goods. As with the GATT reforms, achieving agreement could be done only through a high-level global conference that recognizes the magnitude of the crisis that is building up.

SERVICES TRADE

Of the thirteen types of service industry covered by trade agreements only distribution services, financial services and environmental services pose any great problems. The liberalization of telecommunications services and transport services offers significant benefits to developing countries as well as developed ones, but with nothing to be gained from bargaining over them in trade negotiations. In both cases the regulatory needs are specific to the industry. Transport is so closely linked to trade that the WTO might well be the most appropriate institution to manage it, but not through GATS.

The short-term benefits to developing countries of liberalizing most of the others (construction, energy, business, education, health, cultural, sporting and tourism) are smaller than is often claimed, but there is little to be lost from lumping them together and trading liberalization of one for liberalization of another. Services negotiations should be separate from those on manufacturing and agriculture, but most of these individual service types may not need to be separated from each other. When a country decides what to offer in return for what it can gain it needs to be aware of the potential impacts and exercise a degree of caution. In general the risks are fairly low. For distribution services the risks are higher, with potentially large adverse social effects and significant environmental ones. Financial services and environmental services should both be excluded from the agenda.

Financial services are in great need of stronger regulation, particularly national regulation (Rodrik 2009). To the extent that global regulation needs to be strengthened as well it should not be through GATS and not through the WTO. Whatever mechanisms might be developed to restore and preserve the stability of national and global financial systems, they need to be devoted specifically to that purpose and not subjected to market access demands. Environmental services such as water supply, sanitation and solid waste disposal provide an essential public service for the citizens of each country. They need effective regulation by the government of that country, with no need for any kind of international regulation. Financial assistance from donor countries can be highly beneficial, but with no strings attached for either privatization or liberalization. Liberalization offers potential environmental benefits but can have large social costs if a government does not have the necessary regulatory capacity or the political motivation to apply it. Pressures or incentives to liberalize serve only to increase the chance that it will be done unnecessarily and done badly. Environmental services should be removed completely from the liberalization agenda.

The bargaining power through which high-income countries promote the liberalization of financial and environmental services comes mainly from the single undertaking. If a high-level global agreement were able to dismantle the single undertaking it would have little extra difficulty in revising GATS.

THE SINGAPORE ISSUES AND INTELLECTUAL PROPERTY

Of the four Singapore issues only one, trade facilitation, presents no major problems. The economic benefits of including facilitation measures in a trade agreement are often vastly overstated, but such agreements can be a useful mechanism for organizing cooperative action and international assistance.

The other three issues raised at Singapore did not proceed to negotiations in the WTO, with widespread agreement that the developing countries were right to reject them (Stiglitz and Charlton 2005; Sachs 2005). They should be resisted just as strongly in regional and bilateral agreements. Any short-term gain that might be won by trading them for something else is likely to be more than outweighed by the longer-term losses. Developing countries that genuinely want to develop need to keep control of their own government procurement policies and competition policies, and not concede any more rights to foreign investors than they already have.

If the TRIPs agreement had been proposed at Singapore instead of in the Uruguay Round that too may well have been rejected. An international mechanism for extending intellectual property rights beyond national legislation to take fuller advantage of global markets already existed in the World Intellectual Property Organization (WIPO). Developing countries with little intellectual property to protect had good reason not to go as far as developed ones in granting rights to other countries' companies. They were only persuaded to do so by the leverage that could be brought to bear in the WTO. If the WTO's single undertaking were now dismantled as part of a comprehensive reform, TRIPs could and should go back to WIPO. Developing countries that feel they have no need of it would then be free to extract themselves, in much the same way as for GATT.

In many respects WIPO is the equivalent of GATT in being an institution whose agreements a country needs to adopt once it has reached an appropriate level of industrial development, but not before. The revisions to the TRIPs provisions on generic medicines benefit people in developing countries, but were adopted only because of pressures brought to bear by the industrialized countries' own civil society organizations. The poorer developing countries have little influence to be lost by withdrawing from the agreement.

For intellectual property rights in genetic materials, biodiversity-rich developing countries are in a stronger bargaining position. Neither they nor the industrialized countries whose companies claim rights have shown much interest in conserving biodiversity, either through the WTO or in the overlapping negotiations of the UN Convention on Biological Diversity. Instead they bargain with each other over the profit to be made from creating and allocating monopoly rights in exploiting the resources. The fault lies primarily with the CBD. The WTO is a trade institution, not an environmental one. It has no mandate to conserve biological diversity. The CBD does. It has failed to develop international law that is sufficiently precise to place binding constraints on the WTO. The CBD was established at the 1992 Rio conference, which was itself limited in its ability to constrain neoliberal economic objectives. A new high-level global conference to tackle the economic crisis and the environmental crisis as an integrated whole would be in a position to reverse that. It would need to give the CBD the power to define rules on the use of genetic resources that are binding on all countries, with which the WTO and WIPO would have to comply.

BEYOND RIO AND BRETTON WOODS

Agenda 21, the global action plan agreed at the 1992 world conference in Rio de Janeiro, began with the words 'humanity stands at a defining moment in history' (United Nations 1992: 1.1). The moment cannot last much longer. Some of the plan's actions were implemented but the most important ones were not. Global biodiversity is declining even faster, climate change has been allowed to accelerate, and the needs of the world's poor are still unmet. Rio sought to integrate environment and development alongside economic goals in policy decisions and failed. The same economic policies remained in place until they self-destructed, plunging the world even deeper into crisis. This brief moment in history seems to be getting closer and closer to defining a future that would be extremely unpleasant. Yet there is a silver lining. Neoliberalism is in retreat.

It is well beyond the scope of this book to suggest what kind of new New Deal might fill the vacuum, except that it has to be a global deal, and has to address the economic crisis, the climate crisis, the energy crisis, the ecological crisis, the food crisis and the poverty crisis as an integrated whole (Nadal 2008). A new Bretton Woods is not enough. It has to be a newly combined Bretton Rio. The global conference that puts it in place would not be attended by environment ministers, trade ministers or finance ministers, but by presidents and prime ministers, advised by their entire governments and globally respected experts in every relevant discipline. It would not be one of several conferences addressing separate issues, but the only such conference, setting the ground rules for any subordinate ones until updated by another that is equally comprehensive. Like Bretton Woods it would make concrete commitments, preceded by many months or even years of painstaking preparation and hard bargaining. Much of the bargaining may have to be behind closed doors between the diplomatic representatives of the major players. The key players that paved the way for Bretton Woods were Britain, as the strongest of the old global powers, and the USA, the strongest of the new ones. The corresponding key players who must pave the way for a new Bretton Rio, behind closed doors if necessary, are the USA and China. Europe will have its say, along with India, Brazil, Russia and others, but any global agreement is likely to be critically dependent on agreement between those two.

Climate change would be high on the agenda, aiming in particular for a global emissions control regime that establishes, directly or indirectly, a high enough carbon price to have real effect.[18] The 'polluter pays' principle agreed at Rio can be a powerful way of halting environmental degradation, but cannot be fully effective unless, directly or indirectly, the polluter pays the polluted. When the impact is global the payment has to be global. The money raised from taxes on carbon and other greenhouse gas emissions should in principle go into a global fund spent on global objectives, the most obvious of which is the preservation of rainforests and other biodiversity-rich carbon sinks.

Once a fully effective global mechanism for containing climate change is in place the increase in emissions that would come from fully implementing GATT would be just one small component of an overall balance in which total global emissions are kept within bounds. The reforms discussed above would address most of the other impacts that the international trade regime has on economies, environments and people, but with one major exception. Nothing in the current trade agenda even begins to address the corrupting effect that trade in oil, diamonds and other valuable natural resources can have on the economies, governance systems and development prospects of the countries that possess them. The resource curse goes unrecognized in trade negotiations, because the barriers to trade are few. The buyers want to buy, the sellers want to sell, and the people who suffer have no say. This too should go on the agenda for a definitive world conference, to be negotiated in parallel with the energy crisis and the climate crisis. What better way to solve all three than through a global carbon taxation fund that not only buys up the world's rainforests, but buys its oil extraction rights as well? The elites that currently control them might be bought off at a price far below their total economic value, with enough money left in the fund to invest in the diversification of their countries' economies and in the socio-economic development of their people.

Nothing so gloriously idealistic could be achieved in one go, if ever. Even so, the thinkers who advise presidents and prime ministers should devote a large part of their thinking to their ultimate goal. Globalization has proved to be a fanciful goal in its neoliberal sense, but need not be rejected totally. The world's climate, its rainforests, its seas, its minerals and its oil are all precious global resources that cannot be managed effectively without being managed globally. Adam Smith had no faith in global ideals, but Adam Smith had no telephone and no TV, no access to the Internet, no aeroplanes, and not the slightest knowledge of the technologies that can fly them from continent to continent on the power of the sun. The world is on the cusp of finding ways of governing itself other than perpetual warfare between competing states, competing ideologies and competing beliefs. If we let it fall apart now it will be hundreds of years, maybe thousands, before our descendants get another chance.

12 | AN END AND A BEGINNING

It often requires, perhaps, the highest effort of political wisdom to determine when a real patriot ought to support and endeavour to re-establish the authority of the old system, and when he ought to give way to the more daring, but often dangerous spirit of innovation. (Smith 1982 [1759]: 242)

We begin this concluding chapter with a summary of the main impacts of trade liberalization and its historical context, and go on to review the global context surrounding the proposed reforms. The current international trade regime belongs in an era that is now drawing to its end. The reforms that we discussed in the previous chapter are part of building a new one.

THE IMPACTS

When the trade impact assessment studies began in 1999 we had no idea that they would expand into a ten-year programme, and little comprehension of what the findings might be. Some have been surprising, others less so. The sharpest lessons have come not from examining the economic, social and environmental effects of trade agreements, but from talking to negotiators, reading what they write and watching them at work. They are all good people, whatever countries they represent, and that is the first problem. They are all first-class negotiators, for their own countries, or for particular interest groups within those countries. They do an excellent job of gaining as much as they can while giving as little as possible in return, making use of whatever economic bargaining power they have got. Some have more power than others and gain more than they lose. For others, it is the other way round. At the end of a day's work the ones who have gained the most for whoever they represent sleep soundly, confident of an economic theory which tells them that, whatever has been negotiated, it needs only to have liberalized something somewhere for everyone to be a winner. That, of course, is the second problem.

The theory in which trade negotiators place their faith takes no account of environmental effects, nor of different impacts on different social groups. It is generally assumed that provided there is a net economic benefit, it can be allocated to rectifying any such problem through some other policy. Whether or not that is true, the social and environmental damage cannot be rectified if there is no net benefit.

The theory of comparative advantage on which the ideal of free trade is based has several weaknesses but is basically sound. When David Ricardo identified it he had no way of calculating the size of the effect, but now we do. The computer programs that are used to solve the equations have their own limitations but give a rough indication. Measured in billions of dollars, the welfare gains are big. Compared with the size of the world economy and the amount by which it would normally grow in the time it takes to negotiate and implement a trade agreement, they are insignificantly small.

The minimal overall benefit is the result of much bigger changes in the structure of each country's economy. In the countries that drive the process the changes are consistent with their development strategy and the adjustment is relatively painless. In others, particularly the poorest, the adverse effects are big and the predicted adjustment may never happen.

China, India, Brazil and the newly industrialized developing countries of South-East Asia generally win as much as they lose. The biggest losers are the countries that failed to get on to the development ladder before liberalization took hold. For them the adverse long-term impacts are even bigger than those occurring in the short to medium term. Every liberalizing measure that is agreed, whether for reducing tariffs, removing subsidies, opening services markets, granting rights for intellectual property or adopting other standardized policies, reduces a country's ability to define its own policies for its own development. Again, liberalization is justified on the basis of a simple economic theory, in this case the neoliberal theory of minimal government intervention in the market. Whereas David Ricardo's theory is basically sound but has little effect, this one is basically unsound and has massive effects. It hampers a country's ability to pursue the very agricultural policies that have proved so successful in reducing poverty in South-East Asia and now China. It stops them pursuing the very industrial policies through which the developed countries developed.

Ha-Joon Chang calls it 'kicking away the ladder' (Chang 2002). We should not be too shocked by it. Trade negotiators do it in relatively good faith, following Adam Smith's advice to care for the interests of their own country while trusting the gods of economic orthodoxy to take care of the universe. Every political entity whose wealth has been based on an international trading system has behaved in much the same way. The British and other European empires did it, as did those of the ancient Romans, Greeks, Persians and Babylonians, and the tribute systems of the great Chinese dynasties. All believed that their dynasty would last for ever.

When the Berlin Wall was falling Francis Fukuyama saw it as the beginning of the end of history (Fukuyama 1992). Having demonstrated its superiority over Soviet totalitarianism, the Western ideal would go on to universal and everlasting triumph. Fukuyama's former teacher Samuel Huntington begged to differ. In his eyes the West had gained its pre-eminence not through the superiority of its ideas but through its superiority in applying organized violence. The ending of the cold war would make little difference to a history that would carry on as before, starting with a series of potential clashes between Western civilization and those other civilizations it had temporarily suppressed (Huntington 1997). If Fukuyama were wrong and Huntington were right, the worst of the clashes would be global and somewhat bigger than before, along with the parallel effects of climate change.

The trade liberalization agenda is a neoliberal agenda. It implicitly assumes that Fukuyama's vision of the globally free market as the ultimate end of history was right. It is now clear that Fukuyama was wrong in his deference to the economic orthodoxy, but not necessarily in his hope that the world might finally overcome the worst of its historical tendencies. The challenge we now face is to seize the silver lining in the current economic crisis and make it the deciding factor. Neoliberalism is not the force it was.

A NEW BEGINNING

Countries have always traded with each other and always will. Whatever other benefits international trade might confer it allows people to enjoy precious resources that are not available on or under their own soil, such as silk, gold, coffee and oil. It provides an easy way for local elites to reap the benefit. International trade can, at its worst, be controlled by the most powerful states to secure those resources for their own ends, and employ the rest of the world's people for those ends, whether or not they transport them in chains or import them as slaves. At its best, it is one of the most powerful drivers of human understanding and human development. The current global trade regime is part one, part the other.

The West is now nearing the end of a 300-year period in which it has been the dominant force in the world. Its imperial history is already over, but it remains at the core of an international trading system that was established through that history. The periphery is still poor but large parts of it are getting richer. The West has good reason to congratulate itself on that. Some of its ideals have proved to be genuinely universal human ideals. Although some of the rungs of the development ladder have been removed others have not. Some have been consciously put in place. In some parts of the world their aim has been achieved. Impoverished people are becoming more affluent. The consequences are hard for the West to accept.

The relative decline of Western economic power is occurring at the very same time as exponentially growing exploitation of environmental resources is approaching global limits. The clearance of forests for timber and agriculture has reached the point where biological diversity is becoming dangerously low. Atmospheric pollution has begun to change the whole world's climate, and is doing so increasingly rapidly. Even if that were not enough reason to halt and reverse growing consumption of oil and natural gas, it will soon be replaced by the inescapable reason that supply of the finite resource is nearing its peak. The age of cheap energy is over. New technologies have made solar power more versatile than when people first dried their washing in the sun, water power more efficient than when they first made a water wheel, and wind power more adaptable than when they first set sail, but to imagine that renewable energy can ever take the place of the past century's fossil-fuel bonanza, let alone expand it to provide the same amount of power to over six billion people, is nothing but an idle dream. It is not just people's energy-dependent lifestyles which have to change. Their energy-dependent economic structures have to change, and change radically.

The difficulty is compounded by the West having to accept that it cannot stay in charge for much longer. Samuel Huntington may have been wrong in the worst of his fears, but he was almost certainly right in suggesting that unless the West is prepared to fight another round of wars, with sufficient might to win, it must relinquish much of its power. If it is to do that voluntarily and graciously it must relinquish its monopoly of ideas. It has forgotten that its own Age of Enlightenment was its age of empire-building and slavery. It teaches the rest of the world that democracy brings affluence, while forgetting that its own history was the other way round. Those of us born and bred in the West have become accustomed to teaching other people, and have forgotten how to learn from them. A peaceable world cannot be ruled by Western ideas alone.[19]

In one crucial way the West's ideas of how a polity of many millions of people should be governed are very similar to those of its strongest challengers. America, China, India and Brazil are all federal states, while the European Union is built on similar principles. In governing themselves, all of them endeavour to apply the principle of subsidiarity. What can be managed locally should be. Anything that can be managed only at a higher level must be. Very few things need to be managed globally. They include mineral resources of global importance, the global atmosphere, global biodiversity, and certain specific aspects of international trade. In most other respects countries with different climates, different geographies, different histories and different cultures can be free to govern themselves however they like.

If we had begun the book with the principle of subsidiarity we need not have bothered with all the rest. We would have reached the same conclusions on how the WTO should be reformed as those we discussed in the previous chapter. Assessing the likely impacts of reinforcing the current trade regime has merely confirmed that over-governing people has adverse impacts on them, while under-governing those things on which they all depend results in damaging effects on them all. There would have been no need to demonstrate the inadequacies of neoliberal economic theory. We would have dismissed it as irrelevant. Nevertheless, we would have had to acknowledge from the start that applying the principle of subsidiarity at the global level is a massive challenge for us all.

Many proposals for reforming global governance would be even harder to achieve. David Held advocates a cosmopolitan, social democratic, global ideal as a replacement for the neoliberal global ideal (Held 2004). Anne-Marie Slaughter and Thomas Hale have no more faith in global ideals than Adam Smith, and propose instead a stronger role for trans-governmental networks (Slaughter and Hale 2005). Many of these already exist, covering areas such as financial regulation, environmental protection and counterterrorism. They all need to sharpen their focus on the global essentials. Xu Mingqi and Wu Yikang have identified precisely what those essentials are: global political and security issues such as nuclear weapons and terrorism; global economic issues such as energy supply, financial stability and poverty; and global environmental issues such as climate change (Xu Mingqi and Wu Yikang 2001). They do not include imposing global rules on how a country should conduct its trade policy. Some of the current trade rules deal with critical global issues and are much needed. The rest are not.

At some point in the distant future the ideal of globally free trade might become both practicable and desirable, not for any effect it might have on economic efficiency or growth, but as a guarantor of peace.

The growth that trade liberalization sparks is a fleeting flame, coming to an end when liberalization has achieved its end. Fully free trade can do better than that, but not yet. As in the Union that Europe made of itself after centuries of conflict and two world wars, it can secure the peace only if it means what it says, with free movement of people as well as goods, services and capital. It will be a long while before the world is ready for that. Poor countries have to become nearly as rich as the richest before the borders can be thrown open. Even more than in the construction of Europe's Union, some will need considerable help. Removing the constraints that are currently applied in the name of free trade will not be enough. To lift the world out of its multiple crises all of us, on every continent, need to combine our old ideas into radically new ones that can build a future unlike anything that has ever gone before.

If we succeed in doing that we will have proved Adam Smith wrong, not in his economic theory, but in the forlornly parochial top tier of his moral philosophy. It may have been true in the eighteenth century but not in the twenty-first. The people of this planet will have shown that, for the first time in history, they have developed the capability to communicate with each other, understand each other and like each other enough to value their common interest above their local tribal interests.

NOTES

1 Many civil society organizations have been highly supportive of the impact assessment studies but have criticized them for not going far enough in supporting their own arguments. A joint statement by EU civil society organizations (Friends of the Earth 2006) summarizes their main criticisms as: (1) disconnection from trade policy and decision-making (failure to incorporate SIA findings into EU negotiating positions); (2) weak and inadequate enhancement, prevention and mitigation measures; (3) pro-liberalization bias (failure to question the assumption that trade liberalization is desirable); (4) pro-neutrality bias (failure to assess the relative significance of positive and negative impacts); (5) insufficient stakeholder consultation in third countries; (6) economistic bias (insufficiently influenced by non-economic disciplines).

2 The European Commission publishes positioning papers giving its response to the final reports of the studies (see Chapter 10). The Commission's comments and suggestions for amendments to unpublished draft reports remain confidential.

3 An evaluation of the regulatory impact assessment systems in the European Commission and EU member states found many examples of where impact assessments had been used to make a case for particular proposals rather than to carry out a realistic appraisal of alternative options (Jacob et al. 2008). A review of the UK RIA system by the National Audit Office found several cases in which the assessment had not influenced the decision at all. For example, the National Minimum Wage RIA presented a decision that had already been taken, the Transport Safety Regulation RIA worded the objective in such a way as to close off alternative options, and the RIA for amending the Motor Vehicles (Tests) Regulations merely presented a decision to increase fees in line with inflation (NAO 2006).

4 All of the sustainability impact assessment reports are published on the Euopean Commission's website, ec.europa.eu/trade/issues/global/sia/studies.htm (accessed 25 May 2009). The studies for the WTO Doha negotiations are summarized in Kirkpatrick et al. 2006a.

5 These estimates are derived from Polaski 2006; Laird et al. 2006; François et al. 2005; de Córdoba and Vanzetti 2005. For the studies that modelled less than full liberalization the results were scaled up in proportion to the estimated welfare changes.

6 Some modellers have used an extreme set of assumptions to give an outer bound of the possible magnitude of the overall gain in static economic welfare. These also give an outer bound of the possible production changes. For the removal of tariffs between the EU and Mediterranean countries Patricia Augier and Michael Gasiorek (2001) found that production increased in the EU and Israel and decreased in every manufacturing

sector in every other country except Turkey, where production rose in only one sector. In Egypt the decline ranged from 28 per cent for chemicals and plastics up to 85 per cent for electrical machinery, 95 per cent for wood products, 97 per cent for food, beverages and tobacco and 99.7 per cent for textiles, clothing, leather goods and footwear. Tunisia and Morocco fared little better.

7 From ILO statistics quoted in Polaski 2006.

8 The data used in these estimates are from Bode et al. 2002 and Hertel and Keeney 2006.

9 Senator Mike Huckabee, US presidential candidate, speaking on CNN during the 2008 election campaign. Senator Hubert H. Humphrey, subsequently vice-president, was even more outspoken. In promoting the US Food for Peace Program he observed that 'if you are looking for a way to get people to lean on you and to be dependent on you, in terms of their cooperation with you, it seems to me that food dependence would be terrific' (quoted in Lappé et al. 1977: 343).

10 The estimates are derived from Polaski 2006; Anderson et al. 2006; Sumner 2006; François et al. 2005; Azzoni et al. 2005; FAPRI 2002. For the studies that modelled less than full liberalization the results were scaled up in proportion to the estimated welfare changes.

11 The Master said, 'The requisites of government are that there be sufficiency of food, sufficiency of military equipment, and the confidence of the people in their ruler.' Tsze-kung said, 'If it cannot be helped, and one of these must be dispensed with, which of the three should be forgone first?' 'The military equipment,' said the Master. Confucius (1893 [c.500 BC]).

12 Doornbosch and Steenblik 2007; Crutzen et al. 2007. Crutzen

et al. examined the emissions of nitrous oxide (a particularly powerful greenhouse gas) from the nitrogen used in synthetic fertilizers. They found that for many biofuels, such as the biodiesel produced from rapeseed in Europe, the emissions could contribute more to global warming than the cooling from the savings in fossil fuels.

13 Alfred Marshall, *Principles of Economics*, first published 1890, 8th edn 1920, Macmillan, London, bk VI, ch. XII, p. 15, www.econlib.org/library/ Marshall/marP.html.

14 See the discussion of investment agreements in Chapter 8.

15 From a different perspective Magda Shahin argues that the inclusion of specific standards governing non-trade matters would open a Pandora's box undermining the WTO system itself (Shahin 2009).

16 Jagdish Bhagwati condemns any departure from the ideal of free trade whether pursued by anti-globalization protesters or Western governments (Bhagwati 2002).

17 The positioning papers giving the EC's responses to the impact assessment studies are published on ec.europa.eu/trade/issues/global/sia/ studies.htm (accessed 30 May 2009).

18 The *Stern Review on the Economics of Climate Change* examined the advantages and disadvantages of a variety of approaches to effective international collective action, including both regulatory and economic instruments and various combinations. The report argues that, whatever the approach, it needs to establish an actual or implicit carbon price that is broadly similar throughout the world (Stern 2006). The use of market instruments alone can have major adverse effects on social justice by pricing energy above what is affordable to low-income consumers. Various

forms of energy rationing through the allocation of per-capita quotas have been proposed to counter this (Starkey and Anderson 2005; Fleming 2007).

19 The need for a new global Age of Enlightenment to take the place of Europe's outdated one is discussed more fully in George (2007).

BIBLIOGRAPHY

Abbott, F. M. (2002) 'WTO TRIPs agreement and its implications for access to medicines in developing countries', CIPR Study Paper 2, London: Commission on Intellectual Property Rights.

ActionAid (2007) 'The World Bank and agriculture: a critical review of the World Bank's World Development Report 2008', Johannesburg: Action Aid.

Ali, M. (ed.) (2004) 'Agricultural diversification and international competitiveness', Report of the APO Study Meeting on Agricultural Diversification and International Competitiveness, Tokyo, 16–23 May 2001, Tokyo: Asian Productivity Organization.

Amsden, A. H. (1997) 'Bringing production back in – understanding government's economic role in late industrialization', World Development, 25(4): 469–80.

Anderson, K., W. Martin and D. van der Mensbrugghe (2006) 'Market and welfare implications of Doha reform scenarios', in K. Anderson and W. Martin (eds), Agricultural Trade Reform and the Doha Development Agenda, Washington, DC: Palgrave Macmillan and the World Bank.

Arkell, J. and M. Johnson (2005) 'Sustainability impact assessment of proposed WTO negotiations: final report for the Distribution Services Study', International Trade and Services Policy and University of Manchester.

Arvis, J.-F., M. A. Mustra, J. Panzer, L. Ojala and T. Naula (2007) 'Connecting to compete: trade logistics in the global economy', Washington, DC: World Bank.

Augier, P. and M. Gasiorek (2001) 'Trade liberalization between southern Mediterranean and the EU: the sectoral impact', Discussion Paper no. 79, University of Sussex at Brighton, July.

Auty, R. M. (2000) 'How natural resources affect economic development', Development Policy Review, 18: 347–64.

Azzoni, C., J. Guilhoto, E. Haddad and F. Silveira (2005) 'Agriculture, the case of Brazil', in O. Morrissey, D. W. te Velde, I. Gillson and S. Wiggins, Sustainability Impact Assessment of Proposed WTO Negotiations: Final Report for the Agriculture Sector Study, Overseas Development Institute and University of Manchester.

Bacon, Francis (1597), De Hæresibus, Meditationes Sacrae, in J. Spedding, R. Leslie Ellis and D. Denon Heath (eds), The Works of Francis Bacon, Boston, MA: Houghton, Mifflin, www.archive.org, accessed 30 May 2009.

Balanyá, B., B. Brennan, O. Hoedeman, S. Kishimoto and P. Terhorst (eds) (2005) 'Reclaiming public water: achievements, struggles and visions from around the world', Netherlands: Transnational Institute and Corporate Europe Observatory.

Batie, S. S. and D. E. Ervin (2001) 'Transgenic crops and the environment: missing markets and public roles', *Environment and Development Economics*, 6: 435–57.

Bhagwati, J. (2002) *Free Trade Today*, Princeton, NJ: Princeton University Press.

Bird, G. and R. S. Rajan (2001) 'Banks, financial liberalization and financial crises in emerging markets', *The World Economy*, 24(7): 889–910.

Bode, S., J. Isensee, K. Krause and A. Michaelowa (2002) 'Climate policy: analysis of ecological, technical and economic implications for international maritime transport', *International Journal of Maritime Economics*, 4.

Brunnermeier, S. and A. Levinson (2004) 'Examining the evidence on environmental regulations and industry location', *Journal of Environment and Development*, 13(1): 6–41.

Cali, M. (2007) 'Scale and types of funds for aid for trade', Negotiation Advisory Brief no. 15, Toronto: International Lawyers and Economists Against Poverty.

CEAS (2000) 'Study on the relationship between the agreement on TRIPs and biodiversity related issues', Final report for DG TRADE European Commission, Wye: Centre for European Agricultural Studies.

CENTAD (2008) 'Lamy sees consensus forming for financial rules', *Trade News*, New Delhi: Centre for Trade and Development, 22 October.

Chandra, R. (2003) 'Social services and the GATS: key issues and concerns', *World Development*, 31(12): 1997–2012.

Chang, H.-J. (2002) *Kicking Away the Ladder; Development Strategy in Historical Perspective*, London: Anthem Press.

Choi, H.-S. (1979) 'Technology for development: the South Korean experience', in J. Ramesh and C. Weiss (eds), *Mobilizing Technology for World Development*, New York: Praeger.

— (1986) 'Science and technology policies for industrialization of developing countries', *Technological Forecasting and Social Change*, 29: 225–39.

CIPR (2002) *Integrating Intellectual Property Rights and Development Policy*, Report of the Commission on Intellectual Property Rights, London: CIPR.

Clarke, G., K. Kosec and S. Wallsten (2004) 'Has private participation in water and sewerage improved coverage? Empirical evidence from Latin America', World Bank Policy Research Working Paper no. 3445, Washington, DC: World Bank.

Confucius (1893 [c.500 BC]) *The Analects*, Book 12, trans. James Legge, Clarendon Press, online edition, nothingistic.org.

Contreras, P. and S. Yi (2004) 'Internationalization of financial services in Asia-Pacific and the western hemisphere', Paper presented at the 2nd annual conference of the Pacific Economic Cooperation Council Finance Forum, Hua Hin, Thailand, 8–9 July 2003.

Cororaton C. B., J. Cockburn and E. Corong (2006) 'Doha scenarios, trade reforms, and poverty in the Philippines: a CGE analysis', in T. W. Hertel and L. A. Winters (eds), *Poverty and the WTO: Impacts of the Doha Development Agenda*, Washington, DC: Palgrave Macmillan and the World Bank.

Cosbey, A. (2005) 'International investment agreements and sustainable development: achieving the

Millennium Development Goals', Winnipeg: International Institute for Sustainable Development.

Costa, P. T. M. (2009) 'Fighting forced labour: the example of Brazil', Geneva: International Labour Office.

Cotula, L., S. Vermeulen, R. Leonard and J. Keeley (2009) 'Land grab or development opportunity? Agricultural investment and international land deals in Africa', London/Rome: IIED/FAO/IFAD.

Council of the European Union (2007) 'EU strategy on aid for trade: enhancing EU support for trade-related needs in developing countries', Brussels.

Crutzen, P. J., A. R. Mosier, K. A. Smith and W. Winiwarter (2007) 'N$_2$O release from fertilizer use in biofuel production', *Atmos. Chem. Phys. Discuss.*, 7: 11191–205.

Damill, M. and R. Frenkel (2003) 'Argentina: macroeconomic performance and crisis', Paper prepared for the Macroeconomic Policy Task Force of the International Policy Dialogue, IPD, Barcelona, 2–3 June.

Daniel, B. C. and J. B. Jones (2006) 'Financial liberalization and banking crises in emerging economies', Department of Economics, University at Albany.

Das, B. L. (2002) 'The New Work Programme of the WTO', Penang: Third World Network.

De Córdoba, F. S. and D. Vanzetti (2005) 'Now what? Searching for a solution to the WTO industrial tariffs negotiations', in UNCTAD, *Coping with Trade Reform: Implications of the WTO Industrial Tariff Negotiations for Developing Countries*, Geneva: United Nations Conference on Trade and Development.

Decreux, Y. and L. Fontagné (2006) 'A quantitative assessment of the outcome of the Doha development agenda', CEPII Working Paper no. 2006-10, Paris: Centre d'Etudes Prospectives et d'Information Internationales.

Delich, V. (2002) 'Developing countries and the WTO dispute settlement system', in B. Hoekman, M. Mattoo and P. English (eds), *Development, Trade, and the WTO: A Handbook*, Washington, DC: World Bank.

Development Solutions (2009) 'Trade sustainability impact assessment (SIA) of the EU–Libya Free Trade Agreement', Beijing: Development Solutions.

Dihel, N. (2002) 'Quantification of costs to national welfare from barriers to services trade: a literature review', OECD Trade Committee, TD/TC/WP(2000)24/FINAL.

Dollar, D. and A. Kraay (2000) 'Growth is good for the poor', Policy research working paper no. 2587, Washington, DC: Development Research Group, World Bank.

— (2004) 'Trade, growth, and poverty', *Economic Journal*, 114: F22–F49.

Doornbosch, R. and R. Steenblik (2007) 'Biofuels: is the cure worse than the disease?', Report SG/SD/RT(2007)3, Paris: OECD.

Dutfield, G. (2002) 'Sharing the benefits of biodiversity: is there a role for the patent system?', *Journal of World Intellectual Property*, 5(6): 1–23.

— (2004) 'Does one size fit all?', *Harvard International Review*, 26(2): 50.

Ecofair (2007) 'The World Bank's WDR 2008: agriculture for development: response from a slow trade – sound farming perspective', Discussion Paper no. 10, Berlin/Aachen: Heinrich Boell Stiftung/Misereor.

Economist (2008a), 'How to smite Smoot', 27 March.

— (2008b), 'The battle of Smoot-Hawley', 18 December.

— (2009a) 'The return of economic nationalism', 5 February.

— (2009b) 'Outsourcing's third wave', 23 May.

EJF (2005) 'White gold: the true cost of cotton', London: Environmental Justice Foundation.

Ekins, P. and T. Voituriez (eds) (2009) *Trade, Globalization and Sustainability Impact Assessment*, London: Earthscan.

Emini C. A., J. Cockburn and B. Decaluwé (2006) 'The poverty impacts of the Doha round in Cameroon: the role of tax policy', in T. W. Hertel and L. A. Winters (eds), *Poverty and the WTO: Impacts of the Doha Development Agenda*, Washington, DC: Palgrave Macmillan and the World Bank.

EMPA (2006) Minutes of EuroMediterranean Parliamentary Assembly Committee on Economic and Financial Issues, Social Affairs and Education, Lisbon, 30 January, Brussels: EuroMediterranean Parliamentary Assembly.

Estache, A. and M. Rossi (2002) 'How different is the efficiency of public and private water companies in Asia?', *World Bank Economic Review*, 16(1): 139–48.

Estudio López Dardaine (2009) 'Mercosur exporters' perspective', in Trade Sustainability Impact Assessment (SIA) of the Association Agreement under Negotiation between the European Community and Mercosur: Sector Study for Trade Facilitation, Manchester: Impact Assessment Research Centre, University of Manchester.

European Commission (2001a) 'A sustainable Europe for a better world: a European Union strategy for sustainable development', COM(2001) 264, Brussels.

— (2001b) 'Green Paper: promoting a European framework for Corporate Social Responsibility', COM(2001) 366, Brussels.

— (2002a) 'Communication from the Commission concerning Corporate Social Responsibility: a business contribution to sustainable development', COM(2002) 347, Brussels.

— (2002b) 'Communication by the European Communities and their Member States to the TRIPs Council on the review of Article 27.3(b) of the TRIPs Agreement, and the relationship between the TRIPs Agreement and the Convention on Biological Diversity (CBD) and the protection of traditional knowledge and folklore: a concept paper', Brussels.

— (2003a) 'Proceedings of EC seminar on SIA of trade agreements – making trade sustainable?', Brussels, 6–7 February, trade.ec.europa.eu/doclib/docs/2006/september/tradoc_130035.11.pdf, accessed 22 May 2009.

— (2003b) 'The World Summit on Sustainable Development one year on: implementing our commitments', COM(2003) 829, Brussels.

— (2003c) 'The EC's proposal for modalities in the WTO agriculture negotiations', Brussels, 27 January.

— (2004a) 'Facing the challenge: the Lisbon strategy for growth and employment: report from the High Level Group chaired by Wim Kok', Brussels.

— (2004b) 'A report on the functioning of public procurement markets in the EU: benefits from the application of EU Directives and challenges for the future', Brussels.

— (2005a) 'Working together for growth and jobs: a new start for the

Lisbon Strategy', COM (2005) 24, Brussels.

— (2005b) 'Strategy for the enforcement of Intellectual Property Rights in third countries', Directorate General for Trade, Brussels.

— (2006a) 'Sustainable trade: observations on trade and protectionism', Speech by Peter Mandelson at the External Trade Stocktaking Conference on Trade Sustainability Impact Assessments, Brussels, 21 March, ec.europa.eu/commission_barroso/ashton/speeches_articles/sppm087_en.htm, accessed 23 May 2009.

— (2006b) 'Global Europe: competing in the world: a contribution to the EU's growth and jobs strategy', Communication from the Commission to the Council, the European Parliament and the Committee of the Regions, COM (2006) 567, Brussels.

European Parliament (2006) 'Report on the construction of the Euro-Mediterranean free-trade zone', Committee on International Trade, 2006/2173(INI) Final A6-0468/2006, Brussels.

Evenett, S. and B. Hoekman (2005) 'International cooperation and the reform of public procurement policies', Policy Research Working Paper 3720, Washington, DC: World Bank.

FAPRI (2002) 'The Doha Round of the World Trade Organization: appraising further liberalization of agricultural markets', Working Paper 02-WP 317, Ames, IA: Food and Agricultural Policy Research Institute, Iowa State University and University of Missouri-Columbia.

Finger, K. M. and L. Schuknecht (1999) 'Trade, finance and financial crises', Special Studies, 3, Geneva: WTO.

Finger, M. J. (2006) 'Aid-for-trade:

bonanza for consultants, nothing for development', Trading Up, New Delhi: Centre for Trade & Development, October–December.

Fink, C., A. Mattoo and I. C. Neagu (2002) 'Trade in international maritime services: how much does policy matter?', World Bank Economic Review, 16(1): 81–108.

Fleming, D. (2007) Energy and the Common Purpose: Descending the Energy Staircase with Tradable Energy Quotas (TEQs), 3rd edn, London: Lean Economy Collection.

François, J., H. van Meijl and F. van Tongeren (2005) 'Trade liberalization in the Doha Development Round', Economic Policy, April, pp. 349–91.

Friends of the Earth (2006) 'EU trade sustainability impact assessments: a critical view', Statement of European Civil Society Organizations to the European Commission, October 2006: Friends of the Earth Europe; World Economy, Ecology and Development (WEED); Both Ends; War on Want; WWF; Women in Development Europe (WIDE); Greenpeace; Birdlife International; Germanwatch; Wemos Foundation; Christian Aid; Friends of the Earth Denmark (NOAH); Fairtrade, www.foeeurope.org/publications/2006/siastatement_eucivilsociety_oct2006.pdf, accessed 8 July 2009.

Fukuyama, F. (1992) The End of History and the Last Man, London: Penguin.

George, C. (2007) 'Sustainable development and global governance', Journal of Environment and Development, 16(1): 102–5.

George, C. and B. Goldsmith (2006) 'Impact assessment of trade-related policies and agreements: experience and challenges', Impact Assessment and Project Appraisal, 24(4): 254–8.

George, C. and C. Kirkpatrick (2003) 'Sustainability impact assessment of proposed WTO negotiations: preliminary overview of potential impacts of the Doha agenda: assessment of individual trade measures', Institute for Development Policy and Management, University of Manchester, trade.ec.europa.eu/doclib/docs/2005/january/tradoc_121226.pdf, accessed 30 May 2009.

— (2004) 'Trade and development: assessing the impact of trade liberalization on sustainable development', *Journal of World Trade*, 38(3): 441–69.

— (2009) 'Creation of processes: sustainability impact assessments', in D. Tussie (ed.), *The Politics of Trade*, Herndon, VA: Brill.

GRAIN (2005) 'Bilateral agreements imposing TRIPS-plus intellectual property rights on biodiversity in developing countries', Barcelona: GRAIN, www.grain.org/go/bilats-tp, accessed 6 June 2007.

Grossman, P. (2002) 'The effects of free trade on development, democracy and environmental protection', *Sociological Enquiry*, 72(1): 131–50.

Haakonsson, S. J. and L. A. Richey (2007) 'TRIPs and public health: the Doha Declaration and Africa', *Development Policy Review*, 25(1): 71–90.

Harris-White, B. (2003) *India Working: Essays on Society and Economy*, Cambridge: Cambridge University Press.

Hausmann, R., L. Pritchett and D. Rodrik (2004) 'Growth accelerations', NBER Working Paper 10566, Cambridge, MA.

Hausmann, R., D. Rodrik and A. Velasco (2004) 'Growth diagnostics', Cambridge, MA: John F. Kennedy School of Government.

Held, D. (2004) *Global Covenant: The Social Democratic Alternative to the Washington Consensus*, Cambridge: Polity Press.

Helpman, E. (2004) 'The mystery of economic growth', Cambridge, MA: Harvard University Press.

Hertel, T. W. and R. Keeney (2006) 'What is at stake: the relative importance of import barriers, export subsidies, and domestic support', in K. Anderson and W. Martin (eds), *Agricultural Trade Reform and the Doha Development Agenda*, Washington, DC: Palgrave Macmillan and the World Bank.

Higgott, R. and H. Weber (2005) 'GATS in context: development, an evolving Lex Mercatoria and the Doha Agenda', *Review of International Political Economy*, 12(3): 434–55.

Hilary, J. (2004) 'Trade liberalization, poverty and the WTO: assessing the realities', in H. Katrak and R. Strange, *The WTO and Developing Countries*, Basingstoke: Palgrave Macmillan.

Hodge, J. (2002) 'Liberalization of Trade in Services in developing countries', in B. Hoekman, M. Mattoo and P. English (eds), *Development, Trade, and the WTO: A Handbook*, Washington, DC: World Bank.

Hoekman, B. (2001), 'Strengthening the global trade architecture for development', Development Research Group, Washington, DC: World Bank.

Hoekman, B. and P. Holmes (1999) 'Competition policy, developing countries and the World Trade Organization', Policy Research Working Paper 2211, Washington, DC: Development Research Group, World Bank.

Hoekman, B. and K. Saggi (2002) 'Multilateral disciplines and national investment policies', in B. Hoekman, M. Mattoo and P. English (eds), *Development, Trade, and the WTO: A Handbook*, Washington, DC: World Bank.

Hoekman, B., C. Michalopoulos and L. A. Winters (2004) 'Special and differential treatment of developing countries in the WTO: moving forward after Cancún', *World Economy*, 27(4): 481–506.

Hoque, M. Z. (2003) 'Experimental alternate option to privatization of water industry in Dhaka, Bangladesh', Paper presented at the Third World Water Forum, 16–23 March, Kyoto.

Huckabee, M. (2008) CNN Ballot Bowl, 16 February, transcripts.cnn.com/TRANSCRIPTS/0802/16/cnr.05.html, accessed 27 May 2009.

Hudec, R. E. (2002) 'The adequacy of WTO dispute settlement remedies: a developing country perspective', in B. Hoekman, M. Mattoo and P. English (eds), *Development, Trade, and the WTO: A Handbook*, Washington, DC: World Bank.

Huntington, S. P. (1997) *The Clash of Civilizations and the Remaking of World Order*, New York: Simon & Schuster.

IAASTD (2009a) *Agriculture at a Crossroads*, vol. 3: *Latin America and the Caribbean*, International Assessment of Agricultural Science and Technology for Development, Washington, DC: Island Press.

— (2009b) *Agriculture at a Crossroads: Global Summary for Decision Makers*, International Assessment of Agricultural Science and Technology for Development, Washington, DC: Island Press.

IARC (2007a) 'Update of the overall preliminary trade SIA EU–Mercosur: final report', Impact Assessment Research Centre, University of Manchester.

— (2007b) 'Sustainability impact assessment of the Euro-Mediterranean Free Trade Area: final report of the SIA-EMFTA Project', Impact Assessment Research Centre, University of Manchester.

ICFTU (2002) 'Behind the wire: anti-union repression in the Export Processing Zones', Brussels: International Confederation of Free Trade Unions.

— (2003) 'Annual survey of violation of trade union rights 2003', Brussels: International Confederation of Free Trade Unions.

IMF (2005) 'Dealing with the revenue consequences of trade reform', Washington, DC: Fiscal Affairs Department, International Monetary Fund.

— (2008) 'Global Financial Stability Report 2008: containing systemic risks and restoring financial soundness', Washington, DC: International Monetary Fund.

International Competition Network (2005) 'Building blocks for effective anti-cartel regimes: defining hard core cartel conduct – effective institutions – effective penalties', ICN Working Group on Cartels, Luxembourg: EC Publications Office.

Jacob, K., J. Hertin, P. Hjerp, C. Radaelli, A. Meuwese, O. Wolf, C. Pacchi and K. Rennings (2008) 'Improving the practice of impact assessment', Berlin: EVIA Project.

Jalilian, H., C. Kirkpatrick and D. Parker (2007) 'The impact of regulation on economic growth in developing countries: a cross-section analysis', *World Development*, 35(1): 87–103.

Jansen, M. and A. Keck (2004) 'National environmental policies and multilateral trade rules', Staff Working Paper ERSD-2004-01, Geneva: Economic Research and

Statistics Division, World Trade Organization.

Jha, V. (2006) 'Export orientation of economy and women empowerment: empirical evidence', Paper presented at the Conference on Gender in Global and Regional Trade Policy: Contrasting Views and New Research, University of Warwick, 5–7 April.

Jomo, K. S. (2005) 'Developmental states in the face of globalization: Southeast Asia in comparative East Asian perspective', UNESCO International Seminar, Rio de Janeiro, 8–13 October.

Keck A. and P. Low (2004) 'Special and differential treatment in the WTO: why, when and how?', Staff Working Paper ERSD-2004-03, Geneva: World Trade Organization.

Key, S. J. (1999) 'Trade liberalization and prudential regulation: the international framework for financial services', *International Affairs*, 75(1): 61–75.

Keynes, J. M. (1963 [1930]) 'Economic possibilities for our grandchildren', in *Essays in Persuasion*, New York: Norton, pp. 358–73.

Khan, B. (2008) 'An economic history of patent institutions', in R. Whaples (ed.), *EH.Net Encyclopedia*, eh.net/encyclopedia/article/khan. patents, accessed 30 May 2009.

Khor, M. (1997) 'The WTO and the South: implications and recent developments', TWE no. 161, Penang: Third World Network.

— (2007) 'Bilateral and regional Free Trade Agreements: some critical elements and development implications', UNDP Regional Trade Workshop, Penang, 17–18 December.

Kirkpatrick, C. and W. Watanabe (2006) 'The impact of environmental regulation on Japanese foreign investment in developing countries', Impact Assessment Research Centre Working Paper, University of Manchester.

Kirkpatrick, C., C. George and S. Scrieciu (2004) 'The implications of trade and investment liberalization for sustainable development: review of literature', Report for UK-DEFRA, Impact Assessment Research Centre, University of Manchester.

— (2006a) 'Sustainability impact assessment of proposed WTO negotiations: final global overview trade SIA of the Doha development agenda: final report', Institute for Development Policy and Management, University of Manchester.

— (2006b) 'Trade liberalization in environmental services: why so little progress?', *Global Economy Journal*, 6(2).

Kirkpatrick, C., N. Lee and O. Morrissey (1999) 'WTO New Round: Sustainability Impact Assessment Study Phase One', Institute for Development Policy and Management, University of Manchester.

Kleen, P. and S. Page (2005) 'Special and differential treatment of developing countries in the World Trade Organization', Global Development Studies no. 2, Stockholm: Ministry for Foreign Affairs.

Kleih, U., P. Greenhalgh and A. Marter (2006) 'Sustainability impact assessment of proposed WTO negotiations: final report for Fisheries Sector Study', Natural Resources Institute and University of Manchester.

Koshy, R. (2006) 'Transforming aid for trade: from mirage to reality', *Trading Up*, New Delhi: Centre for Trade & Development, October–December.

Kowalski, P. (2005) 'Impact of changes in tariffs on developing countries' government revenue', OECD Trade Policy Working Paper no. 18.

Krugman, P. (1997) 'What should trade negotiators negotiate about?', *Journal of Economic Literature*, XXXV: 113–20.

Kumar, K. (1978) *Prophecy and Progress: The Sociology of Industrial and Post-Industrial Society*, Harmondsworth: Penguin.

Laird, S. (2002) 'A round by any other name: the WTO agenda after Doha', *Development Policy Review*, 19(2): 41–62.

Laird S., D. Vanzetti and S. F. de Córdoba (2006) 'Smoke and mirrors: making sense of the WTO industrial tariff negotiations', Policy Issues in International Trade and Commodities, Study Series no. 30, New York and Geneva: UNCTAD.

Lall, S. and M. Theubal (1998) 'Market-stimulating technology policies in developing countries: a framework with examples from East Asia', *World Development*, 26(8): 1369–85.

Lappé, F. M., J. Collins and C. Fowler (1977) *Food First: Beyond the Myth of Scarcity*, Boston, MA: Houghton Mifflin.

Levenstein, M., V. Suslow and L. Oswald (2003) 'International price-fixing cartels and developing countries: a discussion of effects and policy remedies', Working Paper 53, Amherst: Political Economy Research Institute, University of Massachusetts.

List, F. (1885) *The National System of Political Economy*, trans. Sampson S. Lloyd, Online Library of Liberty, London: Longmans, Green and Co. (first published in German 1841).

Lobina, E. and D. Hall (1999) 'Public sector alternatives to water supply and sewerage privatization: case studies', London: Public Services International Research Unit.

Machiavelli, N. (1515) *The Prince*, trans. W. K. Marriott, electronic version by J. Roland and D. Stone, Constitution Society.

Mattoo, A. (2005) 'Services in a development round: three goals and three proposals', *Journal of World Trade*, 39(6): 1223–38.

Mavroidis, P. C. (2000) 'Trade and environment after the shrimps–turtles litigation', *Journal of World Trade*, 34(1): 73–83.

McCalman, P. (2002) 'The Doha agenda and intellectual property rights', Manila: Asian Development Bank.

— (2005) 'Who enjoys "TRIPs" abroad? An empirical analysis of intellectual property rights in the Uruguay Round', *Canadian Journal of Economics*, 38(2): 574–603.

Mehta, L. and B. la Cour Madsen (2005) 'Is the WTO after your water? The General Agreement on Trade in Services (GATS) and poor people's right to water', *Natural Resources Forum*, 29: 154–64.

Mill, J. S. (1909 [1848]) *The Principles of Political Economy with some of their Applications to Social Philosophy*, 7th edn, ed. W. J. Ashley, London: Longmans, Green and Co.

Mishra, V. (2002) 'TRIPS, pharmaceuticals and health: a third world perspective', Newsletter 2, Rotterdam: EU-LDC Network.

Molina, N. and P. Chowla (2008) 'The World Bank and water privatization: public money down the drain', Update 62, London: Bretton Woods Project.

Moser, P. (2003) quoted by T. Riordan in 'A stroll through patent history', *New York Times*, 29 September.

Motaal, D. A. (2008) 'The biofuels landscape: is there a role for the WTO?', *Journal of World Trade*, 42(1): 61–86.

Murshed, S. M. (2002) 'On natural resource abundance and under-development', The Hague: Institute of Social Studies.

Nadal, A. (2008) 'Redesigning the world's trading system for environmentally sustainable development', in K. P. Gallagher (ed.), *Handbook on Trade and the Environment*, Cheltenham: Edward Elgar.

Nagarajan, N. (1999) 'The millennium round: an economic appraisal', ECFIN Economics Papers no. 139, Brussels: European Commission.

NAO (National Audit Office) (2006) 'Evaluation of regulatory impact assessments 2005-06', London: The Stationery Office.

Nelson, P. and M. Ryder (2007) 'Trade SIA of the Association Agreement under negotiation between the European Community and Mercosur: Forestry Sector Study', Manchester: Land Use Consultants and University of Manchester.

Odell, J. and S. Sell (2006) 'Reframing the issue: the WTO coalition on intellectual property and public health, 2001', in J. S. Odell (ed.), *Negotiating Trade: Developing Countries in the WTO and NAFTA*, Cambridge: Cambridge University Press.

Odell, J. S. (2006) (ed.) *Negotiating Trade: Developing Countries in the WTO and NAFTA*, Cambridge: Cambridge University Press.

OECD (1998) 'Council recommendation concerning effective action against hard core cartels', Paris: OECD.

— (2002) 'The size of government procurement markets', Paris: OECD Secretariat.

— (2005) 'Trade adjustment costs in OECD labour markets: a mountain or a molehill', in *OECD Employment Outlook*, Paris: OECD.

— (2006) 'Environmental perform-ance review of China', Working Party on Environmental Performance, Paris: OECD.

Oxfam (2002a) 'TRIPS and public health: the next battle', Oxfam Briefing Paper 15, Washington, DC: Oxfam International.

— (2002b) 'US bullying on drug patents: one year after Doha', Oxfam Briefing Paper 33, Washington, DC: Oxfam International.

— (2005) 'WTO members should reject bad deal on medicines', Joint statement by NGOs on TRIPS and public health, 3 December, www.cptech.org/ip/wto/p6/ngos12032005.html, accessed 30 May 2009.

— (2007) 'What agenda now for agriculture? A response to the World Development Report 2008', Oxfam.

Ozler, S., K. Yilmaz and E. Taymaz (2004) 'Labor markets and productivity in the process of globalization: firm level evidence from Turkey', ERF Research Report 0403, Egypt: Economic Research Forum for the Arab Countries, Iran and Turkey.

Page, S. (2007) 'Using trade rules to help development: balancing the benefits and costs of the WTO system for developing countries', International Seminar on the New Agenda for International Trade Relations as the Doha Round Draws to an End, Barcelona, 29–30 January.

Pangestu, M. (2002) 'Industrial policy and developing countries', in B. Hoekman, M. Mattoo and P. English (eds), *Development, Trade, and the WTO: A Handbook*, Washington, DC: World Bank.

Plan Bleu (2003) 'Results of the Fiuggi Forum on Advances of Water Demand Management in the Mediterranean: findings and recommendations', Sophia Antipolis: Plan Bleu.

Polaski, S. (2006) 'Winners and losers: impact of the Doha Round on developing countries', Washington, DC: Carnegie Endowment for International Peace.

Pomfret, R. (2006) 'Regional Trade Agreements', in M. Fratianni and A. Rugman (eds), *Regional Economic Integration*, Amsterdam: Elsevier.

PricewaterhouseCoopers (2005) (team leaders N. Boudeville, S. Richardson and J. Krimphoff) 'Sustainability impact assessment (SIA) of the EU–ACP Economic Partnership Agreements, final report on phase two: the agro-industry sector in West Africa and Mauritania; tourism services in the Caribbean; fisheries in the Pacific ACP countries', Neuilly-sur-Seine: PricewaterhouseCoopers Sustainable Business Solutions.

— (2006) (team leaders N. Boudeville, S. Richardson and J. Krimphoff) 'Sustainability impact assessment (SIA) of the EU–ACP Economic Partnership Agreements, final reports on phase three: rules of origin in the Southern African Development Community; horticulture in eastern and southern Africa; financial services in Central Africa', Neuilly-sur-Seine: PricewaterhouseCoopers Sustainable Business Solutions.

— (2007) 'Sustainability impact assessment of the EU–ACP Economic Partnership Agreements: summary of key findings, policy recommendations and lessons learned', Paris: Pricewaterhouse-Coopers France.

PSIRU (2002) 'Water privatization in Africa', London: Public Services International Research Unit.

Radaelli, C. M. (2005) 'Diffusion without convergence: how political context shapes the adoption of regulatory impact assessment', *Journal of European Public Policy*, 12(5): 924–43.

Raghavan, C. (2000) 'The World Trade Organization and its dispute settlement system', Trade and Development Series no. 9, Penang: Third World Network.

Rangnekar, D. (2002) 'Access to genetic resources, gene-based inventions and agriculture', London: Commission on Intellectual Property Rights.

Ravallion, M. (2008) 'Are there lessons for Africa from China's success against poverty?', Policy Research Working Paper 4463, Washington, DC: World Bank.

Reinert, E. S. (2007) *How Rich Countries Got Rich ... and Why Poor Countries Stay Poor*, London: Constable.

Ricardo, D. (2001 [1821]) *On the Principles of Political Economy and Taxation*, 3rd edn, Ontario: Batoche Books.

Risso, S. and A. Wandel (2004) 'Trade and environment: from corporate diktats to democratic and sustainable rules', in *From Cancún to Hong Kong: Challenging Corporate Led Trade Liberalization*, Brussels/Berlin: Seattle to Brussels Network.

Rodrik, D. (2001) 'The global governance of trade as if development really mattered', New York: United Nations Development Programme.

— (2009) 'A Plan B for global finance', *The Economist*, 12 March.

Romer, P. M. (1986) 'Increasing returns and long run growth', *Journal of Political Economy*, 94: 1002–37.

Sachs, J. (2005) 'Investing in development: a practical plan to achieve the Millennium Development Goals', UN Millennium Project, UNDP, London: Earthscan.

Sachs, J. and A. Warner (1995) *Natural Resource Abundance and Economic Growth*, Cambridge, MA: Harvard Institute for International Development.

Sadler, B. (1996) 'Environmental assessment in a changing world: evaluating practice to improve performance', International Study of the Effectiveness of Environmental Assessment, Ottawa: Canadian Environmental Assessment Agency.

Sandbrook, R. (1992) 'From Stockholm to Rio', in J. Quarrie (ed), *Earth Summit '92*, London: Regency Press.

Scoones, I. (2002) 'Agricultural biotechnology and food security: exploring the debate', IDS Working Paper 145, Brighton: Institute for Development Studies.

Scott, N., S. Batchelor, J. Ridley and B. Jorgensen (2004) 'The impact of mobile phones in Africa', London: Commission for Africa.

Scrieciu, S. (2007) 'How useful are computable general equilibrium models in sustainability impact assessment?', in C. George and C. Kirkpatrick (eds), *Impact Assessment and Sustainable Development: European Practice and Experience*, Cheltenham: Edward Elgar.

Sen, A. (1982) *Poverty and Famines: An Essay on Entitlements and Deprivation*, Oxford: Clarendon Press.

Sengenberger, W. (2005) 'Globalization and social progress: the role and impact of international labour standards', Bonn: Friedrich-Ebert-Stiftung.

Seth, K. (2004) 'History and evolution of patent law: international and national perspectives', *Patent and Trade Mark Reporter*, January–June, New Delhi: Amity University Press.

Shadlen, K. (2005) 'Policy space for development in the WTO and beyond: the case of intellectual property rights', Working Paper no. 05-06, Medford, MA: Global Development and Environment Institute, Tufts University.

Shahin, M. (2009) 'To what extent should labor and environmental standards be linked to trade?', *Law and Development Review*, 2(1).

Shiva, V. (2002) 'The real reasons for hunger', 'Worldview', *Observer*, 22 June.

Singh, A. (2004) 'Multilateral competition policy and economic development: a developing country perspective on the European Community proposals', Genenva: UNCTAD.

Singh, A. and R. Dhumale (1999) 'Competition policy, development and developing countries', Trade-Related Agenda, Development and Equity Working Paper 7, Geneva: South Centre.

Singh, J. P. (2006) 'The evolution of national interests: new issues and North–South negotiations during the Uruguay Round', in J. S. Odell (ed.), *Negotiating Trade: Developing countries in the WTO and NAFTA*, Cambridge: Cambridge University Press.

Slaughter, A.-M. and T. N. Hale (2005) 'A covenant to make global governance work', www.openDemocracy.net, accessed 6 June 2009.

Smith, A. (1904 [1776]) *An Inquiry into the Nature and Causes of the Wealth of Nations*, ed. E. Cannan, Online Library of Liberty, London: Methuen.

— (1982 [1759]) *The Theory of Moral Sentiments*, Glasgow edn, ed. D. D. Raphael and A. L. Macfie, Online Library of Liberty, Indianapolis: Liberty Fund.

Spinager, D. (2002) 'Misinterpreted governance: the case of anti-dumping measures', Paper presented to the EU-LDC Network

Conference, Chiang Mai, Thailand, 8–10 December.

Starkey, R. and K. Anderson (2005) 'Domestic tradable quotas: a policy instrument for reducing greenhouse gas emissions from energy use', Technical Report no. 39, Manchester: Tyndall Centre.

Stern, N. (2006) *Stern Review on the Economics of Climate Change*, chaired by Sir Nicholas Stern, HM Treasury, Cambridge: Cambridge University Press.

Stevens, C., (2002) 'The future of Special and Differential Treatment (SDT) for developing countries in the WTO', IDS Working Paper 163, Brighton: Institute for Development Studies.

Stevens, C. and P. Holmes (2005) 'How constraining is GATS?', Paper presented at the ESRC Seminar on Trade in Services, University of Sussex, 1–2 December.

Stiglitz, J. E. (2002) *Globalization and Its Discontents*, London: Penguin.

Stiglitz, J. E. and A. Charlton (2004) 'An agenda for the development round of trade negotiations in the aftermath of Cancún', London: Initiative for Policy Dialogue and Commonwealth Secretariat.

— (2005) *Fair Trade for All*, Oxford: Oxford University Press.

Straus, J. (2008) 'How to break the deadlock preventing a fair and rational use of biodiversity', *Journal of World Intellectual Property*, 11(4): 229–95.

Sumner, D. A. (2006) 'Reducing cotton subsidies: the DDA Cotton Initiative', in K. Anderson and W. Martin (eds), *Agricultural Trade Reform and the Doha Development Agenda*, Washington, DC: Palgrave Macmillan and the World Bank.

Tao Wang and J. Watson (2009) 'Trade, climate change, and sustainability', in *State of the World 2009: Into a Warming World*, Washington, DC: Worldwatch Institute.

Te Velde, D. W. and D. Bezemer (2006) 'Regional integration and foreign direct investment in developing countries', *Transnational Corporations*, 15(2): 41–70.

Te Velde, D. W., M. Cali, A. Hewitt and S. Page (2006) 'A critical assessment of the EU's trade-related assistance to third countries: lessons from the past', Policy Options for the Future, London: Overseas Development Institute.

Thrasher, R. D. and K. P. Gallagher (2008) '21st century trade agreements: implications for long-run development policy', Pardee Paper no. 2, Boston University.

UNCTAD (1997) 'International trade in health services: difficulties and opportunities for developing countries', TD/B/COM.1/EM.1/2, Geneva: United Nations Conference on Trade and Development.

— (2004) *World Investment Report 2004: The Shift towards Services*, New York and Geneva: UNCTAD.

— (2007) *The Least Developed Countries Report 2007*, Geneva: UNCTAD.

UNDP (2003) *Making Global Trade Work for People*, London: Earthscan.

— (2009) *Poverty in Focus*, 18, Brasília: Bureau for Development Policy, United Nations Development Programme.

UNDP/Rockefeller (2003) 'General Agreement on Trade in Services', in *Making Global Trade Work for People*, United Nations Development Programme, the Rockefeller Brothers Fund and the Rockefeller Foundation, London: Earthscan.

UNECA (2004) 'Economic report on Africa 2004: unlocking Africa's trade potential in the global economy', E/ECA/CM.37/6, Kampala:

UN Economic Commission for Africa.

UNEP/IISD (2005) *Environment and Trade – a Handbook*, 2nd edn, Geneva/Winnipeg: United Nations Environment Programme/International Institute for Sustainable Development.

UNIDO (2002) *Industrial Development Report 2002/2003*, New York: United Nations Industrial Development Organization.

United Nations (1992) 'Agenda 21: Report of the United Nations Conference on Environment and Development', Rio de Janeiro.

— (1999) 'World survey on the role of women in development: globalization, gender and work 1999', New York: United Nations.

Van Liemt, G. (2001) 'Some social and welfare aspects of international trade', EU-LDC Network, www.eu-ldc.org.

Wade, R. H. (2003) 'What strategies are viable for developing countries today? The World Trade Organization and the shrinking of development space', *Review of International Political Economy*, 10(4): 621–44.

Ward, B. and R. Dubos (1972) *Only One Earth: The Care and Maintenance of a Small Planet* (Unofficial report commissioned by the secretary-general of the United Nations Conference on the Human Environment), Harmondsworth: Penguin.

Warwick, H. and V. Cann (eds) (2007) *Going Public: Southern Solutions to the Global Water Crisis*, London: World Development Movement.

Watal, J. (2002) 'Implementing the TRIPS Agreement', in B. Hoekman, M. Mattoo and P. English (eds), *Development, Trade, and the WTO: A Handbook*, Washington, DC: World Bank.

WCSDG (2004) 'A fair globalization: creating opportunities for all', Geneva: World Commission on the Social Dimension of Globalization, ILO.

Weisbrot, M. and D. Baker (2005) 'The relative impact of trade liberalization on developing countries', in E. Hershberg and C. Thornton (eds), *The Development Imperative: Toward a People Centered Approach*, New York: Social Science Research Council.

Wood, C. (2003) *Environmental Impact Assessment: A Comparative Review*, 2nd edn, Harlow: Prentice Hall.

World Bank (2001) *Finance for Growth: Policy Choices in a Volatile World*, Oxford: Oxford University Press.

— (2002) *Global Economic Prospects and the Developing Countries 2002: Making Trade Work for the World's Poor*, Washington, DC: World Bank.

— (2003a) *World Development Report 2003: Sustainable Development in a Dynamic World: Transforming Institutions, Growth, and Quality of Life*, World Bank and Oxford University Press.

— (2003b) *Trade, Investment, and Development in the Middle East and North Africa*, Washington, DC: World Bank.

— (2003c) 'Private participation in infrastructure: trends in developing countries in 1990–2001', Washington, DC: World Bank.

— (2007) *World Development Report 2008: Agriculture for Development*, Washington, DC: World Bank.

— (2008) *Doing Business Reports: Trading across Borders*, available at www.doingbusiness.org, accessed 20 June 2008.

— (2009) *World Development Report 2009*, Washington, DC: World Bank.

World Commission on Environment and Development (1987) *Our Common Future*, Oxford: Oxford University Press.

WTO (2002) 'Assessment of trade in

services'. Communication from Thailand TN/S/W/4, Geneva: WTO.

— (2005) 'Joint statement on liberalization of financial services', Communication from Australia, Bahrain, Canada, the European Communities, Japan, Norway, Oman, Panama, Singapore, Switzerland, the Separate Customs Territory of Taiwan, Penghu, Kinmen and Matsu, and the United States, JOB(O5)/17, Geneva: WTO.

— (2006) 'Recommendations of the Task Force on Aid for Trade', WT/AFT/1, Geneva: WTO.

Xu Mingqi and Wu Yikang (2001) 'Globalization and global governance in 2020: our vision on international organizations in 2020', 2020 Global Architecture Conference, Centre for Global Studies, University of Victoria, 29–31 August.

Zarrilli, S. (2002) 'Trade in energy services and the developing countries', Geneva: UNCTAD.

Zussy, N. (1993) 'Chief Seattle speech', Washington State Library, www.synaptic.bc.ca/ejournal/wslibrry.htm, accessed 6 June 2009.

INDEX